Emmanuel Asi has a marvellous appreciation of the charism of Charles de Foucauld. He comes from a little village in Pakistan where his father was the local tailor and a lay catechist. Asi's love ＿ the scriptures comes from the witness and enthusiasm of his ＿ather working among the small Christian communities of his ＿ome region. Fr Asi is in touch with the little people who are try-＿g to deepen their understanding of the Good News of Jesus in ＿ predominantly Muslim society. His book is refreshing, chal-＿ing and exciting. I hope that those who read it will come to a ＿ppreciation of the marvellous event of the Incarnation and ＿t radically changes our lives as the followers of Jesus. I ＿ it is a mirror of the radical newness of the gospel and its ＿e for our ordinary everyday situations.

＿m Murphy, International Team, Jesus Caritas Fraternity of Priests

＿k bring us in Europe a new look, a new vision of the ＿f Nazareth, the little place of the Incarnation. There ＿rdinary of God' becomes ordinary in the life of Jesus, ＿g the poor.

＿s Nazareth today, that place from where nothing good ＿ It is in the heart of our world, and of our mega-cities, ＿f the poorest. Maybe the new human face of God is ＿m there.

— *Jean-Marie Pasquier, Jesus Caritas Fraternity of Priests*

THE HUMAN FACE OF GOD AT NAZARETH

Dedicated to the Little Brothers and Sisters of Jesus,
Jesus Caritas Fraternities,
and other lovers of Charles de Foucauld who follow, live and love
littleness and hiddenness and the radicalism of Nazareth.

Emmanuel Asi

The Human Face of God at Nazareth

A NAZARETH SPIRITUALITY

the columba press

This edition first published in 1998 by
the columba press
55A Spruce Avenue, Stillorgan Industrial Park
Blackrock, Co Dublin

Cover by Bill Bolger
Origination by The Columba Press
Printed in Ireland by Colour Books Ltd, Dublin
ISBN 1 85607 228 2

Published originally in 1993 by Asian Jesus Caritas Publications.

Contents

Preface

'Can anything good come out of Nazareth?'

It all began on top of a hill at the SVD Retreat House in Baguio City, Philippines. About 25 diocesan priests from 10 different countries of Asia and guest priests from Africa and Latin America gathered for the 'Month of Nazareth', an annual tradition of the Jesus Caritas Fraternity of Priests. It was organised by the Asian Chapter of the Fraternity to which I was invited to participate and to facilitate a week-long retreat.

Although I had been associated with the fraternity since 1981, it was my first experience of such a fellowship gathering for a whole month. This event gave birth to the reflections contained in this book.

Obviously, 'Can anything good come out of Nazareth?' is a question and challenge addressed to Jesus of Nazareth and his village. However, theologically it is a radical question posed against the incarnation: How can this be? How can God, so powerful, take upon himself human limitations and powerlessness? How can a transcendental God become historical? How can the divine become human?

The incarnation of God marks indeed the death of many false and untrue gods of traditional theology in the church. The mystery of the incarnation invites us to rediscover God, who gets lost within our theological dogmas, ecclesial structures, liturgical rubrics and church laws.

The God of the incarnation is extraordinarily ordinary. He is human, common, simple, and lay. He is present and recognisable among unimportant persons, insignificant events and profane places. In fact, it is very easy to miss him in his utter simplicity and ordinariness.

It is very important to rediscover the lost God of the incarnation, especially in our world today where power is the name of the game and one's status defines one's spirituality. Paradoxically, in this very culture of race and competition, of progress and technology, people are becoming more poor, oppressed and enslaved. They need to hear again and to relive the Nazareth *Manifesto of Liberation* (Lk 4: 18-21).

The incarnation has its own culture, its own way of life, values and virtues. It has its own spirituality. It is, in fact, a spirituality. Its call for radicalism reaches all believers and followers of Jesus and his gospel. God opted for this culture and its consequences. How did Jesus, Mary, Joseph and the people at Nazareth respond to this culture of the incarnation? How did they grow in the their understanding of it? How did they accept the influences and implications of this culture? The incarnation of God brought radical changes in their theology, spirituality and sociology (ch 3, 4, 5).

The incarnation is 'orthodoxy' and 'orthopraxy' at the same time. It is not merely a subject matter of theology, but of sociology as well. It is not only a dogma of faith to be studied but also a spirituality and a way of life. It is meant to be lived, to be practised. It has concrete implications for Christian discipleship, religious and priestly life. It serves as a measuring rod of our Christian life and an invitation to conversion and revitalisation of our Christian commitment (ch 3, 4, 5).

God incarnated himself in order to redeem and deliver people from their sufferings, slaveries, their pains and groanings (Ex 2:23-3:10), to liberate the captives, to set the down-trodden free (Lk 4:18). But because the God of the incarnation is rejected, he still continues to suffer, to be hungry, a stranger, homeless, naked, imprisoned (Mt 25:42-43). Where the incarnation is resented, resisted and rejected, there misery continues. Therefore, the mystery of the Nazareth and of the incarnation is to be radicalised and relived (ch 7).

I would like to thank the Little Sisters and Brothers of Jesus who through their 'littleness' and 'hiddenness' constantly reminded me of the mystery of the incarnation. I thank my brother priests in Jesus Caritas, both on the international and the Asian level, in whose fellowship I have discovered more and more the mystery of Nazareth. I particularly thank Allen and Klaus for their brotherly appreciation and support. My sincere and heartfelt thanks and appreciation goes also to Marcy who was a dynamic force in having this book prepared and printed. Likewise, I wish to thank Peachy for her generous editorial remarks. May God, who incarnated and lived at Nazareth, bless them with joy and life .

I especially dedicate this book to my father, whose reflective mind and contemplative heart and whose love for the sacred scriptures have made me into a scripture enthusiast too. In his deep but simple Christian orientation he has, unknowingly, initiated me into Nazareth.

Fr Emmanuel Asi
Feast of the Annunciation
Mariamabad, Pakistan, March 25, 1993

Introduction

What is Nazareth?

What did it mean for Jesus and for his human formation, and even faith formation?

What influence had Nazareth on the mission, ministry, spirituality and values of Jesus?

What was the impact of Nazareth, of the atmosphere, of the context of those 30 hidden years, on the life of Jesus?

How did Jesus, in 30 years, discern and discover the signs of the kingdom of God in Nazareth?

What were the hopes, the dreams, the visions and challenges that Jesus, Joseph, and Mary had in Nazareth?

What did it mean for Joseph, for Mary, for the disciples, for Charles de Foucauld, for diocesan priests, and for contemporary, common and ordinary Christians?

What challenges, questions and invitations emerge from Nazareth? What are the implications of the Nazareth experience in our lives? How does it touch the roots of discipleship?

How does it challenge the foundations of our being Christians?

We hope that the answers we shall find to all our questions may reveal to us the implications of the incarnation, of God becoming human in our life, and through us its implications for the society where we live. May they finally lead us to the radicalism of Nazareth which we aim at in this reflection.

Nazareth is one of the best models of spirituality for diocesan priests and for Christian disciples. The characters therein manifest a very active, yet a very contemplative (not monastic) life, of living, sharing and working together.

Nazareth is the place of the incarnation. It is where the Word of God was conceived. It is the place where the Word grows. It is where one learns to respond to the Word of God. Here is where the Word of God is announced and denounced. As the Word of God grows, incarnation grows. Indeed, it is the place of the growth of God, of 'God-growing' in the human person of Jesus. Here, Jesus learned, he listened, he observed. It was the place where he came to a full realisation of his mission. He sharpened his commitment and grew in his dedication in Nazareth.

PART I

Mystery of Nazareth

In exploring the mystery of Nazareth, it is very important to understand the contexts, both historical and geographical, in which Jesus lived and grew. This is important not only to understand Jesus, but also to understand the mystery of the incarnation. Jesus did not just descend from heaven when he was 30 years of age. He spent 30 long years in the province of Galilee in the town of Nazareth. He grew up in a certain history, in a certain political, cultural, social and religious context. And it is this context which influenced his life, which gave a purpose to his mission. It clarified and sharpened his commitment. It is important, therefore, to understand this context; otherwise, we could dogmatise the incarnation and its growth so much that we could miss its message.

It is also very important to know some facts about the province of Galilee in order to understand what was happening around Jesus. What was the political talk that Jesus was hearing everyday? What was his experience of the provincial economy of his time?

WHAT IS MYSTERY?

The word 'mystery' has its roots in the Greek language. In our common usage, its meaning is rather ambiguous. Ordinarily, it means something which is hidden from human minds, something unknown which can never be explored, can never be known. So we say, 'It's a mystery to me. It is beyond me. I can never understand it.' But in the New Testament, the Greek word for mystery is *mysterion*. Its meaning is somewhat different from how we usually use it. It is true that a mystery is something hidden, but it is meant to be discovered. Though it can never be fully exhausted, it can be known. It is something that is not known now, but it is to be lived in life, and it will be revealed and known gradually.

Mystery implies a process of unveiling, unfolding and revealing. It will not be fully revealed all at once, but only little by little. It is something to be explored by faith, responded to in hope and lived in life. It involves a process of growing into it, a process of faith formation. It also involves a process of discovering. It leads us to a growing understanding of self, of society, of history and above all, of God (Lk 2:52). In this sense, the New Testament uses the word 'mystery'.

The human person is a mystery, too. We are a mystery to one another. But slowly, gradually, we are revealed to each other. In this way, all our social relationships are mystery. Marriage is a mystery, and so is friendship and any form of covenant and commitment. Not that we do not understand it at all, nor that it will never be revealed. But the more we live it, the more we respond to it, the more we experience it, the more real and concrete it becomes. We grow into it.

Mystery is a real paradox. For some it is liberating; for others it is a contradiction, a cause and a sign of the rising and falling of many people (Lk 2: 34).

Mystery and history

There is a great connection between mystery and history. That means that God is constantly revealing himself in life realities, in contextual experiences, in the history, in events, in day-to-day happenings, oftentimes in the 'ordinary', sometimes in the 'extraordinary', in persons we meet and in places we visit, hour after hour, in nature around us. God is constantly revealing himself to humans.

History is the on-going incarnation and revelation of God. At times he reveals himself as Creator, Redeemer, Provider. He reveals himself in human history, personal relationships, events and nature, ecology, astrology. He reveals himself in thunder, lightning (Ex 19), in the stillness and silence (Es 14:14; Zech 2:13; Is 3:15; Ps 4:5). God reveals himself in extraordinary events, persons of national and international fame. But the same God also reveals himself among common, simple, ordinary people, places and events.

History is the mystery of God revealing and the human person responding to God's revelation. Nazareth is such a mystery. It is here that God revealed himself in the most common, ordinary, unknown, hidden way. He was so ordinary and simple that he even suffered non-acceptance and rejection among his own. He came among his own and his own accepted him not, but to all who did accept him he gave power to become children of God (Jn 1:10-12).

In this way, history is a sacrament. It is a sacrament of God's grace and God's love, of God's Providence, of God's protection and guidance. Whenever in our life we experience any or all of these through any place, any person, or event, we know that it is God who is inviting us to respond to the mystery.

GALILEE OF THE NATIONS

Hearing that John had been arrested he went back to Galilee, and leaving Nazareth he went and settled in Capernaum, a lakeside town on the borders of Zebulum and Naphtali. In this way the prophecy of Isaiah was to be fulfilled:
Land of Zebulum! Land of Naphtali! Way of the sea on the far side of Jordan, Galilee of the nations! The people that lived in darkness has seen a great light; on those who dwell in the land and shadow of death a light has dawned.
From that moment Jesus began his preaching with the message, 'Repent, for the kingdom of heaven is close at hand'. Mt 4:12-17

In the days of Jesus, political invaders from powerful empires usually conquered lands and then returned to their empire. However, in order to rule the conquered territories, to suppress the revolt of local freedom fighters, and to ensure effective taxation, they appointed local officials as authorities. The Holy Land during Jesus' time was one of these conquered territories of the Roman Empire. It was divided into three provinces: Galilee, Judaea, Samaria.

Galilee of the Gentiles
Why was it called Galilee of the Gentiles? Galilee was a part of the Promised Land. According to the first book of Kings, when Solomon was building the temple, in order to buy wood of cedar and gold for his palace and temple, he gave ten cities of Galilee to the King of Tyre and Sidon (1 Kgs 9:11). Since that time, the Jews who were living in Jerusalem, in the province of Judaea, looked down on the decapolis (Greek word for ten cities), and the Jews living therein. They started calling it Galilee of the Nations or Galilee of the Gentiles. 'In days past, he humbled the land of Zebulum and Naphtali, but in days to come he will confer glory on the Way of the Sea on the far side of Jordan, province of the nations' (Is 9:1).
The province of Galilee looks like a triangle. On the north it touches

the borders of Lebanon and of Syria as well as Mt Hermon. Down below, in the south near Nazareth, is Mt Carmel. The rest of Galilee has many fields and valleys, the most famous of which is Ashderlon, Jezrael. It has many waterfalls and lakes too.

In Jesus' time the only source of living and flowing water in the whole Holy Land was in Galilee. The Holy Land even today is dry. This water coming from Galilee was the only source of life-giving water for the country. On this, the whole fishing industry, agriculture and even drinking water of the people depended. In fact, there was a big fish market here and they were exporting dried fish from the lake of Galilee.

Periphery of the highway

Another importance of Galilee, not only for Palestine but also for the whole of the Middle East, was that the Galilee province was the meeting point of east and west. It was the only dry route between east and west. And this was true during times of war as well as during times of peace. Both the western Greeks and Romans, as well as the Syrians, Babylonians and Persians, who wanted to go to Egypt by road, had to pass through Galilee. Likewise, for the Egyptians to go to the east; they too, had to pass through Galilee.

Galilee was also a military route during war time. Being at the midway, it was the replenishment centre for food and water of the military troops. The province provided national defence through its fields and mountains. Many important and decisive wars were fought there, an example being the war of Mt Meggido.

During times of peace, it served as a business boundary. However, people passing through from one district to another had to pay a heavy passage toll.

Surprisingly, despite its strategic location and important role, Galilee was unknown and unimportant in the history of the Jews and in the history of the Bible. It offered many things to the country: life-giving water resources, military significance during war and peace, a significant highway. And yet, it was unknown in the Old Testament. This is so because it did not produce any important person. No important event in the history of salvation took place there and no political power came out of it.

But Galilee was very rich in comparison to the whole of Holy Land, which was a desert. So many priests possessed estates and properties in

Galilee. They appointed tenants to look after their land and properties, but they themselves lived in the suburbs of Jerusalem. They would go there only to collect the harvests.

Because Galilee was far away from the throne and the temple, from the political and religious power, the people were considered backward, uncivilised, barbaric and unholy. These poor peasants could rarely go for pilgrimage to Jerusalem to attend the seven day celebrations. They were not well-versed in the Torah, and could not follow the Law fully. Sometimes it was called Galilee of the Gentiles and its people called 'the people who lived in darkness, those who dwell in the shadow of death'. Their dialect was different from the pure and sophisticated language of Jerusalem. This is why we read in the passion narratives how Peter was caught because of his accent. The Hebrew he was speaking was noticed by the maid-servant, and she told the soldiers to arrest him for being a Galilean.

Historically, Galilee has no importance either; politically, it has no role to play; and religion-wise, it is far from the temple. It was far from Jerusalem, where political and religious power resided. It was far from the temple and the throne. The only good work that the province was doing was feeding the temple and the throne at Jerusalem, the priest and the king. At that time, Galilee was the only food-producing province in the whole of Palestine. Galilee had to feed the structure of Jerusalem, pay taxes and feed both the throne and the temple.

What a paradox of power! The weaker feeding and giving life to the stronger. Being source of life to the stronger yet still remaining politically unimportant and historically unnoticed! This is the mystery of Galilee. Can anything good come out of Nazareth?

GALILEE AND JESUS

Galilee was the locus of the mission and ministry of Jesus. It was very important in Jesus' life. He was conceived, brought up, and grew in Galilee. He spent thirty years there. He began his teaching and preaching in Galilee (Lk 4:14-15, Mt 4:23-25). And after the resurrection he wanted his apostles to go to Galilee to meet him there (Jn 20).

From the scriptures we see that a greater part of Jesus' life was spent in Galilee. Only the infancy narratives and the passion, death and resurrection accounts took place in Jerusalem. All the other activities of Jesus – preaching, teaching and miracles – took place there. Another

interesting point is that all the apostles were from Galilee. Only Judas
Iscariot was a non-Galilean. And he was the one who let Jesus down.

Many events and miracles in Jesus' life took place in this province.
The first miracle happened in Cana; at Mt Thabor the transfiguration
took place; the confession of Peter happened in Caesarea Philippi. We
find there the Lake of Galilee, and Capernaum – the town of Peter
which later became the second home of Jesus. There is Bethsaida,
Khorizon, the Mt of Beatitudes – which is the place of the multiplication of the loaves and the primacy of Peter; Magdala – the town of
Mary Magdalene; Tiberius, the famous city along the shore of Lake
Galilee; Naim, and of course, Nazareth. It is also good to note that all
the miracles which happened on the boat and are connected with fish
took place in the Lake of Galilee, the only lake in Palestine. This lake is
also called Lake of Genezareth or Lake of Tiberius.

Conclusion

As a conclusion let us ask ourselves:

– Why was Galilee, being part of the Promised Land, called the
Galilee of the Gentiles?

– Why was Galilee, which was at the periphery, not famous, unimportant, a rejected and neglected place in the history of the people,
chosen by God and liked by Jesus to become the central place of his
ministry, teaching and preaching?

– Jesus is also called Galilean, which was not a good title. It was
synonymous with gentile, barbarian, uneducated, uncivilised, unholy.
What fears do we feel when people call us by certain human labels,
limitations or prejudices; when people label us because of our own
cultural and geographical limitations?

– When, where and how have I experienced Galilee in my life?

The experience of Galilee
is an experience of powerlessness in the eyes of the people,
being regarded unimportant and pushed to the periphery,
being far away from the centre,
labelled by prejudices.

Think of such experiences, happenings
and events in your life.
It is only through similar experiences

that we become the possibility of the incarnation
and the medium of God's mission.
When we are neglected by the people,
it is a sign that we are being selected and chosen
to share his experience.
This is what we call the experience
and the mystery of Galilee.

The mystery of Galilee of the Gentiles
is God working in human powerlessness
and in the areas of our life and history
of which we are not proud.

How do we respond to these experiences and mysteries?
How did Jesus respond to the mystery of Nazareth?
Why did Jesus choose the periphery and not the centre?
Why did Jesus choose powerlessness and not the structure of
power?

Where do I stand:
in Jerusalem or in Galilee?
In the centre or at the periphery?
With the powerful or with the powerless?

PART II

Nazareth of the New Testament

NAZARETH OF GALILEE

The next day, after Jesus had decided to leave for Galilee, he met Philip and said, 'Follow me.' Philip came from the same town, Bethsaida, as Andrew and Peter. Philip found Nathanael and said to him, 'We have found the one Moses wrote about in the Law, the one about whom the prophets wrote: he is Jesus son of Joseph, from Nazareth.' 'From Nazareth?' said Nathanael. 'Can anything good come from that place?' 'Come and see,' replied Philip. When Jesus saw Nathanael coming he said of him, 'There is an Israelite who deserves the name, "incapable of deceit".' 'How do you know me?' said Nathanael. 'Before Philip came to call you,' said Jesus 'I saw you under the fig tree.' Nathanael answered, 'Rabbi, you are the Son of God, you are the King of Israel.' Jesus replied, 'You believe that just because I said: I saw you under the fig tree. You will see greater things than that.' And then he added, 'I tell you most solemnly, you will see heaven laid open and, above the Son of Man, the angels of God ascending and descending' Jn 1:43-48.

Nazareth, of what good?

In the gospel according to John, the name of the village of Nazareth was first introduced in the vocation story of the first five disciples, who later became apostles of Jesus. Nazareth is presented as having no charm, no value, not attractive.

Philip was one of those first apostles. A very simple Galilean, he was so happy, excited and thrilled to have met Jesus. We cannot imagine how he must have told the details of this experience to Nathanael; how he found Jesus, the Messiah, the Prophet, and that he is from Nazareth. Nathanael, after listening to him and seeing his enthusiasm, must have told Philip that he was a very good but stupid Galilean. Nathanael was a righteous Jew, faithful and familiar with his traditions and knowledgeable about the scriptures and history. His first human and Jewish reaction was 'Can anything good come out of Nazareth?'

Nathanael advises and admonishes Philip to be a good Jew and to read his history and tradition well. Nazareth is not mentioned anywhere in the scriptures. Nazareth has no prophecy to its name, no contribution of any kind in the cultural, religious and political history of the Holy Land. What good can come out of Nazareth, an unknown, insignificant, and unimportant town? His reaction to Philip reflected a very common human prejudice. Surprisingly, Jesus appreciated Nathanael for being so human and a true, honest and faithful Israelite.

Literal meaning

The word 'Nazareth' has two basic and main meanings:

In Arabic language the root NSR means help, encouragement, support, friend, sharer, co-participant. It also means protection from danger, conqueror, deliverance, liberation, one who causes liberation and brings about freedom by paying the ransom for others.

In the Hebrew language it means freshness, green, blossoming. It also means supervising, taking care of, protecting and providing. It has also connotations of growth, increase and fertility.

Many times in Semitic cultures and languages, names of both persons and places have qualitative meanings, attributes and characteristics. Paradoxically, in spite of such good attributes to its name, both in the Arabic and Hebrew languages, Nazareth remains anonymous, insignificant and unimportant in the Old Testament. Nazareth is not mentioned in the Bible nor in parabiblical Jewish literature, nor in documents outside the Bible.

Archaeologists too, had very little to say about Nazareth. They tell us that there were people living in it during the time of David and Solomon, and that it was inhabited during the Romans' time till the fourth century AD. They also found grinding machines, oil pressures, agricultural tools, and a water reservoir. Nazareth was a fertile, blossoming, food-giving place and an organised village.

The paradox and mystery is that although it had so much to give and contribute, it was not given credit at all. It had so much to offer but was not appreciated. No name. No fame. And this is the fate of Nazareth. Can anything good come out of Nazareth?

PEOPLE AT NAZARETH

Who were the different people at Nazareth during the time of the Holy Family and Jesus? Who were the people who encountered Jesus but who reacted and responded to him very differently than he expected? These people did not recognise the Word of God; they did not accept the Word becoming flesh, God becoming human and growing at Nazareth. They all lead us to the mystery of Nazareth.

There was the family of Jesus, there were his friends and relatives. There were the people who used to come to Jesus' shop. There were teachers and Rabbis who taught him basic Jewish catechism. There were also groups of young, zealous and vigorous Zealots, the freedom fighters who held meetings and talked about the oppression and slavery of the Jews under the Romans. Jesus, as a youth, must have attended these meetings and listened attentively to the proceedings.

Various responses and reactions

Different people had different responses and reactions to the mystery and experience of the incarnation. Many persons are mentioned in the infancy narratives who responded in a variety of ways. The gospel according to Luke begins by mentioning the old, barren, childless, righteous and God-fearing family of Zachariah, the priest, and his wife Elizabeth. Their son, still to be born, jumps and dances with joy upon meeting Jesus in the womb of Mary. The shepherds and the Magi adore and pay homage to the new-born baby. Herod and his court people tremble with fear at the news of his birth and plot to kill him. Simon, the prophet, and the widow Anna, daughter of Phanuel, the prophetess, meet the child Jesus when he is forty days old and call him a Redeemer and prophesy about him.

The most amazing and dramatic response and reaction of acceptance and rejection to the incarnation, however, happened during the first public preaching of Jesus in the synagogue of Nazareth. For Luke, this episode serves as 'programme story', i.e., it summarises what is going to happen later throughout the gospel in the public ministry of Jesus.

In this Lucan programme story, some accepted his message and spoke favourably of him. Some were astonished at his gracious words. They marvelled at the appealing discourse which came from the lips of Jesus (Lk 4:22). At the same time there were also those people who were angry and enraged, those who sprang to their feet, those who rejected him, those who boycotted him, those who cast him out and considered him a dangerous person (Lk 4:29). There were also those who planned to kill him, to throw him down the cliff of the hill (Lk 4:30).

Yes, the Word became flesh and dwelt among us. He came among his own and his own accepted him not. But those who accepted him he empowered to become children of God (John 1:10-12).

Jesus was amazed even more by the reactions and responses of his family members, his village folks. He was amazed at their human pre-judices, their non-acceptance and disrespect for God's incarnation. They were so possessed and enslaved by their human biases that they despised God's grace and divine visitation. 'Where did he get all this? How is it that such miraculous deeds are accomplished by his hands? Is this not the carpenter, the Son of Mary?' … They found him too much for them … He could work no miracles … so much did their lack of faith distress him, that he had the round of the neighbouring villages instead … (Mk 6:1-6).

PLACES AND PRAYERS AT NAZARETH

Nazareth is located in an important part of the province of Galilee. It is halfway on the road from the Lake of Galilee in the east, to Haifa in the west. It is on the southern border of Galilee-Samaria.

Today, there are many historical and biblical places in Nazareth that can be visited. Each place marks an important event which took place there.

Places

The Church of the Annunciation

This is the most dominating and the central building in Nazareth. One gets the impression that this big church is looking after and tak-ing care of the whole village. On this location the incarnation event is believed to have taken place. It is here that the annunciation happened and the angel gave the message to Mary. At the cave of the incarnation, it is written: 'Hic est Verbo caro factum est', 'Here the Word became flesh.'

This beautiful basilica was completed on 25 March 1969, after eight years' work. About a hundred artists from all over the world worked there. On the wall of the courtyard of the church, the Hail Mary is written in various languages of the world.

St Joseph's Church

This is the place where the Holy Family used to live. It is also called the Church of Providence.

Well of Mary

From this well Mary used to get water. This is the oldest well which still gives water today. According to some traditions, the annunciation started at this well. But when Mary looked behind she did not see anyone. She went back home and the rest of the annunciation took place at home. This has to do with the tradition of the Old Testament annunciation stories which usually happens near a well or spring or where water is flowing. In the book of Genesis, most of the patriarchs got good news about their God-arranged marital life at the well.

Synagogue of Nazareth

This is the place where Jesus learned his prayers, his catechism, his Torah, his Jewish laws and where twice he came to preach. On both occasions he was rejected. The most famous event is his reading of the prophet Isaiah and his first public preaching (Lk 4:16-30).

Cliff of the Hill

Outside Nazareth, there's a hill from which the people decided to kill Jesus by throwing him down. This happened after his first preaching and rejection in the synagogue of Nazareth (Lk 4:29-30).

Prayers

The places we have described above show us how God is worshiped and his Word adored in human history. It is in the day-to-day affairs, in the family life, in manual work, in the synagogue that God appears. These places reveal to us some aspects of the mystery of Nazareth. When we visit them today we can read a prayer and one gospel text written at every entrance. The important message of these places is described in that text and prayer.

At the annunciation church, it is written: The Virgin Mary, upon hearing the Word of God said Yes to God in obedience. Because her love of God was true and real, she surrendered her will totally to the will and plan of God.

At St Joseph's church, the following text is written: He emptied himself and assumed the condition of a slave and became as we are (Phil 2:6-7). Under this text, the following interpretation is written:

No one in the history of humankind, because of his background was so misunderstood as Jesus. Being Son of God, he was taken as son of a carpenter. Whoever likes and loves Jesus will have to choose and accept and follow this way.

Pope Paul VI, who made his pilgrimage to the Holy land in 1964, said this prayer:

O town of Nazareth, O town of the carpenter's son, touch us and give us wisdom to discern that submission and labour is needed for dignity, redemption and liberation.

THE IMPORTANCE OF NAZARETH

After Herod's death, the angel of the Lord appeared in a dream to Joseph in Egypt and said, 'Get up, take the child and his mother with you and go back to the land of Israel, for those who wanted to kill the child are dead.' So Joseph got up and, taking the child and his mother with him, went back to the land of Israel. But when he learnt that Archelaus had succeeded his father Herod as ruler of Judaea, he was afraid to go there, and being warned in a dream he left for the region of Galilee. There he settled in a town called Nazareth.

In this way the words spoken through the prophets were to be fulfilled: *He will be called a Nazarene!* Mt 2:19-23

Nazareth, among the many places associated with Jesus, stands out as a silent, powerless and contemplative place. According to the standard of the powerful people, it was a rejected city – a gentile and unholy city. Geographically, Nazareth was at the border of Samaria, and its people were mostly pagan, non-Jew and belonging to a mixed race. Because of this, Orthodox, pious and righteous Jews would consider themselves unholy and impure if they come in touch with the gentiles. Therefore, the righteous Jews will never touch the land and culture of the Samaritans. Remember the astonishment of the Samaritan woman when Jesus asked him for water. 'You are a Jew. How can you ask me, a Samaritan and a woman, for a drink?' And the evangelist adds this note to make it clear: 'The Jews have nothing to do with Samaritans.' (Jn 4:9)

Nazareth was rejected, impure, gentile, unimportant, not famous, and hidden. It is silent because it had no history, no reference, no importance, no voice in history. But it was a special city in the eyes of

God, and it became the place of the incarnation. Here, God came down on earth, in history. It was the Nazareth event which served as the dividing line of human history into BC and AD, and which created what is known as Old Testament and New Testament. Here, God became flesh. Indeed, Nazareth is the holiest spot on earth.

Another importance of Nazareth is that it recalls experiences and reflections of covenant and commitment. It was here that Jesus learned and where he was formed to remain faithful to his call and covenant even if it meant the cross and Calvary. It was in this town of Nazareth that Jesus spent thirty long years of his hidden life, his childhood, boyhood, his youth. Here he prepared for his call, covenant and commitment. From here too, people from all walks of life can learn lessons of commitment, whether it is in the family life, from parents to children, or from children to parents; whether in social life, or in religious life's fidelity to vows. Whatever commitment one may have made – contemplative, prophetic, commitment of brotherhood, mutual understanding, love and service – this Nazareth experience helps us to be faithful to it. Nazareth also reminds us of crosses, sufferings and sacrifices that we have to undergo to remain faithful to our 'Yes', call, covenant, commitment.

Conclusion

Concluding this section and standing in and before the Nazareth experience, we can reflect on the following points:

– Nazareth is a place of no importance in the Jewish history. Here, the Son of God is misunderstood, rejected and not appreciated. But there are other deeper theological points besides.

– At Nazareth, we find a holistic spirituality. There is no dichotomy of the spiritual and the material, the sacred and social life. The gospel is conceived and formed in human experience, in social life, in political realities and in cultural contexts.

– The Word of God grows in me depending on my response. God is there where God is least expected. Can anything good come out of Nazareth?

– And finally, 'Nazareth' is a mystery of life, history, relationships and responses. It is a mystery because slowly, one explores and discovers it. 'Nazareth' is an experience and a spirituality. Nazareth is a way of life. The experience of Nazareth never lets anyone down.

PART III

Annunciation at Nazareth

In the sixth month the angel Gabriel was sent by God to a town in Galilee called Nazareth, to a virgin betrothed to a man named Joseph, of the House of David; and the virgin's name was Mary. He went in and said to her, 'Rejoice, so highly favoured! The Lord is with you.' She was deeply disturbed by these words and asked herself what this greeting could mean, but the angel said to her, 'Mary, do not be afraid; you have won God's favour. Listen! You are to conceive and bear a son, and you must name him Jesus. He will be great and will be called Son of the Most High. The Lord God will give him the throne of his ancestor David; he will rule over the House of Jacob for ever and his reign will have no end.' Mary said to the angel, 'but how can this come about, since I am a virgin?' 'The Holy Spirit will come upon you,' the angel answered, 'and the power of the Most High will cover you with its shadow. And so the child will be holy and will be called son of God. Know this too: your kinswoman Elizabeth has, in her old age, herself conceived a son, and she, whom people called barren, is now in her sixth month, for nothing is impossible to God.' 'I am the handmaid of the Lord,' said Mary, 'let what you have said be done to me.' And the angel left her. Lk 1:26-38

EVENTS AND EXPERIENCES AT NAZARETH

Many events and experiences took place at Nazareth. It was here that God became human, where the Word of God took flesh. It was here that the Word of God grew and matured in thirty years. The following events and experiences either took place at Nazareth or are in relation to Nazareth:

a. Annunciation to Mary	Lk 1:26-38
b. Annunciation to Joseph	Mk 1:18-25
c. Holy family settling in Nazareth	Mt 2:19-

d. Growth at Nazareth	Lk 2:41, 51-52
e. Baptism and Temptation	Mt. 3:13-17,
	Mk 1:9-11
f. Prophetic Preaching at Nazareth	Lk 4:16-30
g. Public Teaching and Healing	Mt 4:23-25,
	Lk 4:14-15
h. Jesus abandons Nazareth	Mt 4:12-13
i. Nazareth re-visited	Mt 13:53-58
j. Apparitions of the Risen Lord	Mt 28:16-20

Among these references to Nazareth, the ones that I personally find most significant are: the annunciation to Mary, the annunciation to Joseph, the prophetic preaching at the Synagogue and Nazareth revisited. It is interesting that out of these four, the first two are stories of annunciation (Word of God accepted) while the last two are about denunciation (Word of God rejected).

ANNUNCIATION TO MARY

This story narrates how God visits and intervenes in human history and calls humanity to respond, participate and collaborate with his plan. Trusting in God's providence and power, one is asked to say 'Yes' no matter how impossible and difficult it may sound and look, according to human standards and limitations.

God's visitation

In the Bible, all 'call' stories and vocation narratives are presented as God's visitation. At every visitation he has deep and lasting messages not only for the persons concerned but for all of us. God wants to tell us at each event that he is interested in human history. He intervenes in human history. This visitation is enacted through his care, concern and his providence for human beings. Through these visitations he wants to remind his people that he is the Emmanuel, 'God with us'. He wants to remind them about, and to renew, the covenant: I will never forget you, I am with you.

An angel is always sent by God to visit different people. But those are not only mere social visits; they are always laden with deep meaning. The theology and spirituality of God's visitation is best explained in three hymns from the Lucan infancy narratives. They are so carefully preserved in church official prayers: The Song of Mary (Lk 1:46-55), The Song of Zachariah (Lk 1:68-79) and the Nunc Dimitis (Lk 2:29-32).

Vocation narrative

The narrative of the annunciation to Mary is similar to that of the vocation narrative in the Old Testament. The human person whom God is visiting and calling, presents his/her human limitations and status. The human limitations are sometimes cultural, at times they are due to heritage, lineage, or are sometimes physical, social or mental in nature.

In Mary's dialogue with the angel, she does not doubt God's power but merely admits her powerlessness, human limitations and incapability. She does not ask questions to reject, but to seek clarification in order to know the message deeply. She does not understand what is happening and what is going to happen. She is awed and bewildered in the presence of God. It is difficult (impossible?) for humans to grasp this. How can this be …?

Many scholars today think that Mary took some months to say her final Yes. Her Yes is not the result of a one-and-a-half-minute dialogue. It is difficult to give such an important and life-long Yes in a hurry. And so she asks: 'How can this be?'

At Nazareth we experience how God works in our world. God asks for human participation in executing the plan of salvation. God asks us to become agents of good news and invites us to become the point of departure of his work. God is asking you and me to present ourselves totally, selflessly and unconditionally to him, to say Yes.

Response to the annunciation

God's incarnation begins with Mary's Yes. She trusts God's grace, his power, his Spirit and his providence in doing the difficult and the impossible. She embraces the grace to respond to the Spirit and to listen to the Word.

But although the incarnation is God's initiative and interest, it asks for our personal response. Incarnation begins also with our Yes. St Bernard has a beautiful reflection on Mary before saying her Yes:

The whole world waits for Mary's answer

You have heard that you shall conceive and bear a son; you have heard that you shall conceive not of man, but of the Holy Spirit. The angel is waiting for your answer; it is time for him to return to God who sent him. We too are waiting, O Lady, for the word of pity, even we who are overwhelmed in wretchedness by the sentence of damnation.

And behold, to you the price of our salvation is offered. If you consent, straightway shall we be freed. In the eternal Word of God were we all made, and lo! we die; by one little word of yours in answer shall we all be made alive.

Adam asks this of you, O loving virgin, poor Adam, exiled as he is from paradise with all his poor wretched children; Abraham begs this of you, and David; this all the holy fathers implore, even your fathers, who themselves are dwelling in the valley of the shadow of death; this the whole world is waiting for, kneeling at your feet.

And rightly so, for on your lips is hanging the consolation of the wretched, the redemption of the captive, the speedy deliverance of all who otherwise are lost; in a word, the salvation of all Adam's children, of all your race.

Answer, O Virgin, answer the angel speedily; rather, through the angel, answer your Lord. Speak the word, and receive the Word; offer what is yours, and conceive what is of God; give what is temporal, and embrace what is eternal.

Why delay? Why tremble? Believe, speak, receive! Let your humility put on boldness, and your modesty be clothed with trust. Not now should your virginal simplicity forget prudence! In this one thing alone, O prudent Virgin, fear not presumption; for although modesty that is silent is pleasing, more needful now is the loving-kindness of your word.

Open, O blessed Virgin, your heart to faith; open your lips to speak; open your bosom to your Maker. Behold! the Desired of all nations is outside, knocking at your door. Oh! if by your delay he should pass by, and again in sorrow you should have to begin to seek for him whom your soul loves! Arise, then, run and open. Arise by faith, run by the devotion of your heart, open by your word. 'And Mary said: Behold the handmaid of the Lord: be it done to me according to your word.'

(From the homilies of St Bernard: *In Praise of the Virgin Mother*)

ANNUNCIATION TO JOSEPH

This is how Jesus Christ came to be born. His Mother Mary was betrothed to Joseph, but before they came to live together she was found to be with child through the Holy Spirit. Her husband Joseph, being a man of honour and wanting to spare her publicly, decided to divorce her informally. He had made up his mind to do this when the angel of the Lord appeared to him in a dream and said, 'Joseph, son of David, do not be afraid to take Mary home as your wife, because she has conceived what is in her by the Holy Spirit. She will give birth to a son and you must name him Jesus, because he is the one who is to save his people from their sins. Now all this took place to fulfill the words spoken by the Lord through the prophet: 'The virgin will conceive and give birth to a son and they will call him Immanuel, a name which means "God-is-with-us".'

When Joseph woke up he did what the angel of the Lord had told him to do; he took his wife to his home and though he had not had intercourse with her, she gave birth to a son; and he named him Jesus. Mt 1:18-25

Although the word Nazareth is not mentioned in this particular event, it is taken for granted that it happened in Nazareth.

Usually when we speak of the annunciation, we speak and remember only the annunciation to Mary. We overlook or do not emphasise enough the annunciation to Joseph. This is one of the many injustices done to Joseph, the carpenter of Nazareth, the husband of Mary. We shall call this text 'the annunciation to Joseph'.

Parallel annunciation story
The annunciation to Joseph is a parallel narrative to the annunciation to Mary. There are strong and significant similarities in these two annunciation narratives. The following could be noted:

Luke's infancy narrative revolves around Mary: a feminine narrative story, while Matthew's infancy narrative revolves around Joseph: a masculine narrative story.

Luke is writing for the Gentiles, (Greeks and Romans) and he is emphasising the motherhood of Mary. On the other hand, Matthew is writing for the Jews, and he wants to emphasise the fatherhood of Joseph and the legality of his fatherhood. He wants also to bring Joseph to protect and safeguard a pregnant virgin.

Another interesting point is the divine-human dialogue that transpired. In Luke, whenever the angel appears, the person to whom the angel is speaking is fully awake and takes active part in the dialogue. There are questions and answers meant to erase the doubts, as well as assurances which remove the fears.

In Matthew, however, whenever the angel appears, the person is asleep. He speaks in a dream; there is no dialogue.

According to the Jews it is only in a dream that God reveals himself. You cannot see God, you can only hear him. If you see God, you will die. So, in Matthew's annunciation narrative, there is no dialogue and hence no questions, no answers. One only has to hear and obey the voice.

Joseph the righteous

We must understand some basic points about Joseph in order to understand, admire and appreciate the great role of Joseph in his response to the annunciation.

Joseph stands in the line of the patriarchs. He has a very important role in the history of salvation. He stands out as a hero of faith. He is called the righteous. Joseph is a silent character in the gospel; we never hear him talking. As a righteous, pious, good Jew, he could have left Mary and could have insulted her as an act of following the Law. At first he decided to do so, but after the angel's message, he obeyed God. In his option, he proved himself a righteous man.

Joseph was caught in a dilemma. Mary was his legal wife, betrothed to him. But she was found pregnant even before coming to live with him. A good Jewish husband had to get rid of somebody like her. There were cultural norms and religious laws that a righteous person had to follow in situations like this. Joseph must leave Mary, insult her- or stone her to death in order to prove and safeguard his righteousness and his piety. If Joseph did not abandon Mary, he would not be obeying the Law. He had to be faithful to his cultural heritage, social status, his righteousness. He should withhold his name from a child whose father he was not.

Consulting the Law, things became clear for Joseph. Everything was laid down in the Law (Deut 22:20). Being a man of integrity, he decided to leave Mary. However, he would not insult her publicly. And that is the human dimension of his being righteous. He suspected that there was something wrong somewhere but he did not understand how. He did not insult Mary in public. Here, we are faced with a different Jew, a completely different Jew. A good Jew, a righteous person in the fullest sense of the word. He wants to follow the Law and at the same time respect the human person. Here is a man who is righteous before the Book, and righteous before God.

He informally decided to leave her and it was only at this crucial and critical time that the angel intervened. Joseph was told: 'Do not be afraid.' The Annunciation to Joseph took place when he decided to divorce Mary informally and leave her, while the annunciation to Mary took place when she decided to be the wife of Joseph.

In both these Annunciation stories, fear goes with the reception of the good news. When the good news is sent by God, fear is a usual reaction by the recipient. Fear to come before God, fear to lose, fear to let go, to let things happen. Actually the greatest fear is fear of self. We are also oftentimes beset with social, cultural and religious fears somehow, somewhere. And these human fears can be the biggest obstacles to the incarnation. We can even have these fears legally dogmatised and culturally well protected. But if we allow them to reign, then the incarnation will never happen. Fear does not allow the incarnation to happen.

Obedience to the divine will

In the annunciation to Joseph, he stands out to be prophetically obedient to God's voice. Joseph made a personal decision to leave Mary as his wife. Now God tells him to change that personal decision and to obey.

God is asking Joseph to break a law. God is teaching him that the Law, no matter how sacred and dogmatic, cannot be higher than the word and the will of God. The problem and difficulty for Joseph is: Whom shall he obey? The Law, the dogma or God? Will he give in to self-esteem, to social pressure, or to the will of God? When in obeying God, one disobeys religious or civil authorities, it is a prophetic disobedience. It is a radical and revolutionising obedience.

The legal structures have laid out very clearly what Joseph as a husband and righteous person ought to do. He is to leave Mary, insult her in public and stone her to death (Jn 8). In doing this, Joseph will prove himself virtuous, pure and righteous. The Law supports insulting human persons in order to prove that one is honourable. Legal authorities clearly tell him: 'Abandon her, stone her to death in public.' But Joseph thinks that God is beyond our knowledge and plans, beyond our projects. His Spirit is beyond our wisdom and insights, and thus Joseph decides to obey God.

It may be an interesting exercise to recall how Joseph is portrayed and depicted in holy pictures and statues in our churches. He is shown journeying, holding the donkey. He is shown carrying or holding Jesus in his arms. He is doing manual work with tools in his carpenter's shop. He is taking care of and protecting the Holy Family.

In all these pictures, Joseph is portrayed as silent and contemplative even when he is shown as active and dynamic. What a fascinating character and what a marvellous response to the incarnation.

Carlo Carretto wrote a book about Mary, entitled *Blessed is she who believed.* I wish somebody could write a book about Joseph: *Blessed is he who believed.* Actually, Carlo Carretto, in that book showed more strongly the faith of Joseph than that of Mary. Culturally, socially and spiritually, those could have been said of Joseph's beliefs too. But he was silent in the scriptures, and therefore often ignored, neglected. This is another proof of his total surrender and submission. Doing all God told him to do and doing it in silence.

In the church life, Joseph is neglected and put at the periphery; he is an underestimated saint. We must devote some time in reflecting on the spirituality of Joseph. What a difficult life it must have been for him! And yet, his life seemed to be peaceful. What could have been the reason behind it?

> This is the general rule that applies to all individual graces given to a rational creature. Whenever divine grace selects someone to receive a particular grace, or some especially favoured position, all the gifts for his state are given to that person, and enrich him abundantly.
>
> This is especially true of that holy man Joseph, the supposed father of our Lord Jesus Christ, and true husband of the queen of the world and of the angels. He was chosen by the eternal Father to be the faithful foster-parent and guardian of the most precious treasure of God, his Son and his spouse. This was the task which he so faithfully carried out. For this, the Lord said of him, 'Good and faithful servant, enter into the joy of your Lord.'
> (Bernardine of Siena)

Conclusion

As a form of conclusion, let us reflect on some personal implications of the annunciation narratives of Mary and Joseph in our lives:

– God is interested in human history, in our personal circumstances. He shows his concern and care for us and comes to visit us.

– All 'extraordinary' events begin with the 'ordinary'. And we must allow these to happen.

– God's grace is greater than human powerlessness, fears, limitations.

– Gestation and growth of the Word of God happens also and

especially among ordinary, simple people and in day-to-day life experiences. It does not happen only in high class, well-organised liturgies and rituals, nor in philosophical dogmas.

– God offers us a constant, on-going invitation to participate and contribute in the salvation of the people and to become agents of the good news.

– God is above and beyond religious laws, social and cultural structures and ecclesial institutions, no matter how holy, how sacred or dogmatic these may be. We must choose God and obey him even at the risk of disobeying human laws and structures.

– Incarnation will take place in our life only with our Yes.

– What are my fears? What doubts, questions, obstacles do I have?

Let our response to the Annunciation be the following prayer:

God, let me trust in your grace and generosity, in your providence and power. Let me allow you to be God in me, to do your Word and your Will in me as Mary and Joseph did. Let me say: let it be, let it go and let it happen. Let what you have said be done to me. Amen.

PART IV

Denunciation at Nazareth

In the scriptures there are two annunciation narratives (accepting of God's word) and two denunciation experiences (rejecting God's word). Both denunciation events happened with Jesus at Nazareth. And on both occasions Jesus was at the synagogue.

PROPHETIC PREACHING AT NAZARETH

Jesus, with the power of the Spirit in him, returned to Galilee; and his reputation spread throughout the countryside. He taught in their synagogues and everyone praised him.

He came to Nazareth, where he had been brought up, and went into the synagogue on the sabbath day as he usually did. He stood up to read, and they handed him the scroll of the prophet Isaiah. Unrolling the scroll he found the place where it is written:

The spirit of the Lord has been given to me, for he has anointed me. He has sent me to bring the good news to the poor, to proclaim liberty to captives and to the blind new sight, to set the downtrodden free, to proclaim the Lord's year of favour.

He then rolled the scroll, gave it back to the assistant and sat down. And all eyes in the synagogue were fixed on him. Then he began to speak to them. 'This text is being fulfilled today even as you listen.' And he won the approval of all, and they were astonished by the gracious words that came from his lips.

They said, 'This is Joseph's son, surely?' But he replied, 'No doubt you will quote me saying, "Physician, heal yourself" and tell me "We have heard all that happened in Capernaum, do the same here in your own countryside".' And he went on, 'I tell you solemnly, no prophet is ever accepted in his own country.'

'There were many widows in Israel, I can assure you, in Elijah's day, when heaven remained shut for three years and six months and a great famine raged throughout the land, but Elijah was not sent to

any one of these; he was sent to a widow at Zarepath, a Sidonian town. And in the prophet Elisha's time there were many lepers in Israel, but none of these was cured, except the Syrian Naaman.'
When they heard this everyone in the synagogue was enraged. They sprang to their feet and hustled him out of the town; and they took him up to the brow of the hill their town was built on, intending to throw him down the cliff, but he slipped through the crowd and walked away Lk 4:16-30.

The above text is called the *Nazareth Manifesto*, the *Charter of the Messianic Kingdom.* Jesus delivered it, so to speak, at the local synagogue on a Sabbath day in the presence of his parents.

Main themes

What called so much attention in Jesus' action and made the people react was not the reading of the prophetic text but the prophetic explanation of what he read. The most astonishing and disturbing part of the whole narrative was when Jesus, after having finished the scripture reading, said.: 'Today, this scripture passage is fulfilled in your hearing' (Lk 4:21). And to this arose serious reactions.

The dominating and central theme in this preaching is worship and justice. This is the most important and central theme of all the prophets, especially the prophets of the eight centuries before Christ. Worship to God and justice to others go hand in hand. A dichotomy between these two themes will lead one easily to hypocrisy or idolatry. In this text we are given a sharp distinction between belief and idolatry. The idea behind it is that faith or spirituality is not a private affair with God.

Spirituality is related to society and faith finds its meaning in contextual realities and in concrete life. This outlook is important and can greatly influence our theology, spirituality and approach to pastoral life. God, who used to be regarded as the All Holy, three times holy and transcendental, who is beyond, has now come in our history. He is in the midst of our society. This gives purpose to our life and meaning to our ministry. It inspires us to get involved in the transformation towards a better society.

The second important theme in this episode is the *kairos* of salvation, the *today* of salvation, its now-ness and presence. Jesus said: today the scripture has been fulfilled in your sight. The *kairos,* the today of salvation has come by and through me. I am the fulfillment of all. As I

am standing before your eyes, this text is being fulfilled. The *today* in
the text has radicalised it. It was like saying: I am the text fulfilled and
the prophecy personified.

The difficulty does not begin with the reading of the word of God,
but with living it, fulfilling it in one's life. And this provokes reaction.
So does the interpretation of the text in our life. In our present generation we do not have only the word, but the concretisation of it. Today
it is not the text of Isaiah that is before us, it is Jesus himself standing in
front of us. The word becomes alive in life. The word becomes flesh. It
is not anymore the text that confronts but the person of Jesus. And this
always provokes serious reaction and response.

REJECTED AMONG HIS OWN

Going from that district, he went to his home town and his disciples accompanied him. With the coming of the sabbath he began
teaching in the synagogue and most of them were astonished when
they heard him. They said, 'Where did the man get all this? What is
this wisdom that has been granted him, and these miracles that are
worked through him? This is the carpenter, surely, the son of Mary,
the brother of James and Joset and Jude and Simon? His sisters,
too, are they not here with us?' And they would not accept him.
And Jesus said to them, 'A prophet is only despised in his own
country, among his own relations and in his own house'; and he
could work no miracle there, though he cured a few sick people by
laying his hands on them. He was amazed at their lack of faith.
Mk 6:1-6

In Galilee, at the synagogue of Nazareth, the preaching of Jesus pro-
voked various reactions and responses: wonder and praise, rejection of
the Word, prophetic interpretation, doubts and crisis, anger and ani-
mosity.

They rejected Jesus; they hated him. But each hateful response is an
act of killing. It is the climax of non-appreciation, non-acceptance.

NAZARETH AND MIDIAN

So Moses was taught all the wisdom of the Egyptians and became a
man with power both in his speech and his actions.
At the age of forty he decided to visit his countrymen, the sons of
Israel. When he saw one of them being ill-treated he went to his
defence and rescued the man by killing the Egyptian. He thought

his brothers realised that through him God would liberate them, but they did not. The next day, when he came across some of them fighting, he tried to reconcile them. 'Friends,' he said 'you are brothers; why are you hurting each other?' But the man who was attacking his fellow countrymen pushed him aside. 'And who appointed you,' he said 'to be our leader and judge? Do you intend to kill me as you killed the Egyptian yesterday?' Moses fled when he heard this and he went to stay in the land of Midian, where he became the father of two sons. Acts 7: 22-25

At this point, it is interesting to see serious parallelism between the events in Moses' life and that of Jesus. Midian is the place where Moses fled to. Moses was also rejected by his own. Moses was 40 years old and Jesus was 30. Moses and Jesus went to their people with many hopes and expectations to liberate them, and both were confronted with failure and disillusion .

Both of them as missionary, revolutioniser, leader and pastor were rejected on the very first day that they made their public appearance (Acts 7:22-25). Both Jesus and Moses experienced how not to be accepted by their people. They planned and lobbied to kill them. Moses ran away to Midian and Jesus left Nazareth, his home town, and took Capernaum as his second home.

What is the Midian experience?

Midian is an experience of wanting to be liberator and Messiah, but not being accepted by the people. They reject and plan to kill you. You feel that God sends you to be a liberator and a leader, yet your own people resist and reject you. This is death in itself.

Midian is the experience of feeling lonely, of being left alone and rejected. It happens when we find ourselves fighting alone for our commitment and feeling that there is no one with us. This is an experience of feeling one's utter poverty and powerlessness, of being useless, being unsuccessful or unworthy. At this point it seems that all our plans, our visions and our projects are falling apart.

Maybe Moses and Jesus went a little too fast, too quickly, too enthusiastically. Maybe, like many liberators, they wanted a short cut to success. They did not take into consideration that they themselves had to go through certain growth processes. This is a temptation we can have when we are affected by some messianic complex. In one or two years we want to change the situation of our church, our parish, of our community, of the people involved in our project. Maybe we are not listening enough as disciple and evangeliser. Both Jesus and Moses realised that they needed to listen and to learn more.

This is the Midian experience: a desert within us. Both Moses and Jesus went through this desert within them, and decided to go back to their original call. Moses, after the burning bush experience, went back to Egypt after forty years, to the desert with his father in-law. Now he is eighty. Jesus, after having been rejected, went back also after a few months to Nazareth.

THE DARK NIGHT OF JESUS

Jesus has been healing, teaching, preaching all around. Then he went back to Nazareth. Some people in Nazareth were murmuring: What you did in other countries, do it here. He was totally rejected and denounced in his own town among his own people. This rejection is the dark night of Jesus at Nazareth.

Despising God's grace by human prejudices

Once again, it is sabbath day and Jesus is in the synagogue. He is preaching and he gets different responses and reactions. Responses of bewilderment, astonishment. When the people saw Jesus there were questions and doubts, labelling and accusations:

– Where did this man get all his knowledge? He never went to any theological school. What are his theological degrees and credentials?
– What is this wisdom that has been granted to him?
– How to explain these miracles that are worked through him?

They raised questions against Jesus which challenged his wisdom, miracles, and his source of authority in doing all that he was doing. They knew him as the carpenter's son, the son of Mary; and they could not accept that he was more than what they knew him to be. They were more concerned with his origin, with human standards and popular recognition.

On this basis, they utterly rejected him. The result was mutual amazement and astonishment. The people were amazed at the wisdom of Jesus and Jesus was amazed at their lack of it.

No faith, no miracles

In Nazareth, those who had no faith experienced no miracles. Mary and Joseph accepted the word of God and the biggest miracle happened: God came down on earth; God became a human being like us. They responded to and obeyed the word and the will of God. The people of Nazareth lacked fullness of faith and so they saw no miracles. They despised God's grace and the hour of salvation. Salvation came to their own town, to their own houses, but they did not accept it. They did not recognise the time of visitation. Where there is doubt and suspicion, faith is blocked.

The beauty of the incarnation is that it reveals to us that God is simple.and ordinary. He lives among us. At times, we have wrong and high expectations of God, and our religion tries to make him sophisticated and complicated. And so we miss the point of the incarnation. People who are looking for God in academic standards, social stature, moral credentials, cultural, racial, tribal, social, family status, are in for disappointment.

Faith becomes stagnant when God is tied to human standards. We measure God with our dogmas or we try to fit God within our dogmatic puzzles and packages. This is the biggest sin and insult we can do against the incarnation .

Similarly, monopolising God is the exploitation and oppression of God. Sometimes we want to take control of God. We expect him to speak and reveal himself as we desire him to and as it fits us. Why can we not accept the mystery of the incarnation? Why can we not accept that the incarnation can be so simple as a carpenter's son, as the Nazarene? The Jews could not accept this model of the incarnation. If the incarnation had taken place in the temple in Jerusalem, to a priestly family or to a king, and not to a carpenter's son nor to a Nazarene, then perhaps, the people would not have resisted God or resented Jesus.

The 'dark night' in Nazareth

The concept of the 'dark night' is taken from St John of the Cross, a very famous and well-known mystic of the church. He sometimes called it *via negativa*. Dark night means deprivation of light. When it happens to us we don't see any light; we don't know where to go. Every committed believer and prophet, in his/her struggle to be authentic, honest and committed, goes through this and similar experiences. Moses, Jeremiah, Jesus – they all had this experience.

It is a journey of personal wholeness and spiritual integrity. There comes a time in our ministry when we are tempted to quit, to finish, to walk away. We feel hopeless and worthless. And when this happens, many people abandon God and prayer. They abandon friends, even their married partners. Others abandon apostolates, ministries, long standing careers and their community. Some even leave their views and commitments totally behind.

John of the Cross says: 'In fact, the darkness is the place where selfish, romantic egoism dies.' Then the person is set free for God and for the others. The dark night is liberative. It transfigures one's narrow ideas of love and affection. Through this, the selfish idea of love is liberated and transformed.

God, in his loving design, supplements the efforts of the soul by instilling the dark night of deprivation, in order to draw the soul further to intimacy and union with him. The dark night is like an experience of drying and purging. Purging means cleansing or purifying the emotional and sensational, the sensory appetites.

In the dark night, a broken, poor, powerless, rejected and worthless person is invited and led to open up to the mystery of God in love. Once we give up, surrender, submit our powerlessness and worthlessness to God's Spirit, we move into a world of self-esteem, affirmation, compassion and solidarity.

During the dark night, the person experiences a series of transformations. Selfishness is changed into compassion and solidarity. Compassion gives birth to solidarity and identification with the suffering of others. One is enabled to suffer with those who suffer and to celebrate with their liberation. This point is very common and famous among the teachings of Asian mystics. As I am transformed, the ego dies, the 'I' is transformed into 'We'. The lover and the beloved become one.

In the denunciation experience of Jesus at Nazareth, even in his dark night, we are offered a model of growth in grace.

Attachment – detachment

His mother and brothers now arrived and, standing outside, sent in a message asking for him. A crowd was sitting round him at the time the message was passed to him, 'Your mother and brothers and sisters are outside asking for you.' He replied, 'Who are my mother and my brothers?' And looking round at those sitting in a circle about him, he said, 'Here are my mother and my brothers. Anyone who does the will of God, that person is my brother and sister and mother' Mk 3:31-35.

Denounced at Nazareth, Jesus went through the experience of the dark night of the soul. Jesus abandons Nazareth, and detaches himself from his home town, his relatives, friends, dear ones. He overcomes his emotional desires and relational ties. He comes out of the narrowness of Nazareth, of his human idea of family, and moves out of his 'Nazarethness' to universality. The biblical basis of the universal family of God lies in this decision of detachment from one's family ties. The emotional and sentimental attachment to family is changed into universal brotherhood and sisterhood (Mt 12:46-50).

After the tragic event of the denunciation, the word Nazareth is not mentioned anymore in the New Testament, and Jesus does not return there anymore either. Jesus begins to see his own family in the horizon of God's family. His concept of life, which was limited by family and Jewish concepts, is now widened. He learned to detach, to take distance from his closest circle of friends, from his family, and from the socially biased, culturally limited and religiously narrow bindings. He dies to his narrow tribal-like ties and he rises up with his universal love. So he asked these questions:

What is family? What is religion?
Who is my Mother? brother? sister?
Who is related to me and how?

This is the basis of universal brotherhood and sisterhood. Those who listen to and obey the word of God, those who respond to the invitation to incarnate God's word, those who accept grace, these are my brothers and sisters and mothers. My family are those who are one with me in my mission.

Conclusion

From the denunciation at Nazareth let us reflect on some points:

Both the events of denunciation shown in Luke 4 and in Mark 6 happened in the synagogue, at the place of worship, in a holy place. On both occasions, the incarnation was rejected by the synagogue-goers and by the religious leaders of his time.

On both occasions, Jesus was rejected on the basis of human prejudices, social status, cultural and contextual limitations. This is the Nazareth experience: rejection of the incarnation. Jesus was looked down upon, denounced and disowned by his own people.

At Nazareth, God is rejected and denounced because he incarnated in an ordinary and simple way. This is a very important aspect of the incarnation, as was experienced also by Charles de Foucauld. It is the littleness, the hiddenness of God, his being simple and ordinary that they could not accept. The Holy becoming Lay! In so doing, he becomes humanly so unattractive that he is rejected and is denounced.

At this point, it may be helpful to recall when we had last experienced the dark night and the Midian in our life. Maybe it happened when we wanted to become the liberator and Messiah for our people with a fascinating agenda, but the people did not accept our projects and plans and did not believe in our miracles. Then we felt useless, worthless, unsuccessful, without followers. People did not have faith in us. We could not work wonders, no miracles. Then we had the temptation to run away or abandon everything.

This experience of Nazareth and Midian will begin in our life as soon as we start to live the gospel without compromise. We shall surely receive the same responses and reactions as Jesus received when the day comes that we shall be as courageous as Jesus was in proclaiming our mission. Our Midian will come the moment we are able to tell the people with whom we are working that through us the *Kairos,* salvation of this society has come. Today, the scripture text is fulfilled before your eyes. At this point, our Nazareth, our incarnation, and our Midian experiences will surely begin.

The questions we must face are:

– Did the dark night and Midian experience, the desert within, make me more intimate with Jesus or did I become worthless, doubtful of God's providence, power, and grace in me?

– Am I growing in detachment from tribal-like narrow family ties and feelings, passions and desires? This experience of detachment is certainly the pre-requisite, basis and *a priori* condition for the experience of universal brotherhood and sisterhood, of God's family and human love.

Let us now imagine that we are interviewing Jesus, in silence, about his experience of denunciation and his dark night at Nazareth. Try to enter into his feelings and share yours with him. You will understand better the denunciation at Nazareth after sharing your own experience with Jesus and 'listening' to him.

PART V

Virtues and values of Nazareth

They came to Capernaum, and when he was in the house he asked them, 'What were you arguing about on the road?' They said nothing because they had been arguing which of them was the greatest. So he sat down, called the Twelve to him and said, 'If anyone wants to be first, he must make himself last of all and servant of all.' He then took a little child, set him in front of them, put his arms round him, and said to them, 'Anyone who welcomes one of these little children in my name, welcomes me; and anyone who welcomes me welcomes not me but the one who sent me.'...
'But anyone who is an obstacle to bring down one of these little ones who have faith, would be better thrown into the sea with a great millstone round his neck' Mk 9:33-37, 42.

Standing before the Nazareth experience we witnessed and experienced some places, persons, and happenings. But we especially reflected how different persons responded to the word and will of God in Nazareth. Now we shall enter into the life of the Holy Family and discover some human and evangelical values in domestic, social, ordinary life. We will reflect how the Holy Family discerned and discovered the signs of the kingdom of God. How they sowed the seeds of the good news in their own family, in the very ordinary day-to-day domestic life. We must remember that Jesus learned all that he preached about from his home, from the influence of his family in Nazareth.

Little Brother Charles listed the virtues that he learned at Nazareth: faith, hope, charity, chastity, poverty and obedience. Then he categorized values and virtues into two types:
– Inward virtues: humility, courage, truth.
– External/outward: objective work, retreat, penance, prayer.

Values can also be discussed and shared either as personal and individual or as societal and communitarian; and they are innumerable.

These values and virtues serve as our guidelines for living. They express the inner self and our deeper spirituality. Every human person lives by some set of values and virtues which are the essentials of life. Some of these values are inherited from our parents. Some are learned and imbibed from religion; some are sociological, political, family virtues. Some are taught in school, in the religion class. Certain values one is formed into by family and friends. Some are acquired; you grow into them personally or through the influence of others. Acquiring values involves some kind of process of learning and doing, sometimes of unlearning. All these happen in contact with others.

These human values and virtues are the basis and measure of being human. They are also an invitation to live one's Christian call and commitment. To our joy, they coincide with the gospel norms which discipleship demands.

LITTLENESS AND HIDDENNESS

Littleness is the most basic, most important, most impressive, and most attractive value in Nazareth. This was experienced by Jesus, Mary and Joseph in Nazareth. The word 'little', adapted by the little brothers, little sisters and used by Bro Charles, does not refer to self-image. It is rather a very deep expression of spirituality, way of life and of the value and virtue of Nazareth. Brother Charles loved Nazareth because of its littleness, of its powerlessness, of being unknown. What he saw in Nazareth he has adapted as his other name.

The word 'little' as used in the Bible has nothing to do with age, height, or physique. In the cultural context of first-century Palestine, it meant little in status. The little ones are those who are not important, those who have no voice nor vote, those at the periphery. They do not count at all. These are the little ones. So we hear Jesus telling his apostles and disciples to accept them.

God's power in human powerlessness

Hiddenness refers to obscurity. Charles de Foucauld was crazy about finding and living the experience of the hidden life of Jesus at Nazareth – those thirty hidden and obscure years of Jesus' life. He used to say: 'You have to be crazy to love. If you are not crazy, you cannot love.' Hiddenness means not to have ambition for power or social status. It is to be free from social prestige, cultural superiority, economic greed and political pressures.

In the writings of oriental mystics, gurus, bhagat, faqir, a mystic is one who is not indebted to anyone except to God. This is the first step of discipleship, intimacy and deep love. Love of God will become possible only when these evangelical values are lived. It is the surrender of powerlessness before the Most Powerful, the Most Almighty. A believer, a disciple, a follower should become like a straw mattress which is in the prayer place and which is trampled upon by people for twenty-four hours. The parable of the straw mattress at the place of worship is about littleness and hiddenness. It speaks of our surrendering and submission to God's will and word. In powerlessness, littleness and hiddenness, the disciple is always in close intimacy with the Almighty and the Most Powerful.

If we reflect on this virtues of littleness and hidden love, then faith, hope, charity and obedience cease to be diffcult to attain. So littleness and hiddenness is central to the spirituality and charism of Nazareth.

Paschal in practice

This littleness and hiddenness is other-oriented. Littleness means giving little and less to ourselves and being more generous to others. It enables us to share and to give ourselves up for others in order to be free to serve God and the neighbours. In the sense that it is emptying ourselves for God and for the others, then we can say that it is paschal.

Offering ourselves up for others is like making of ourselves a ransom for them. Ransom, in the Old Testament, is given when someone has to pay an amount to liberate somebody. Jesus can be said to have paid himself as ransom to liberate us. To be a ransom is the essence of the paschal mystery. It invites us to offer ourselves to liberate others. Littleness is paschal in practice and experience. It is making real in our lives the death and resurrection of Jesus so that we can be totally for others (Phil 2:6-7).

Mother of various virtues

Littleness and hiddenness give birth to many virtues and values. They can lead to simplicity, which results in generosity. Simplicity as described by Brother Charles is not to have too much nor too little. It asks us to put a limit on our needs. There are various kinds of needs and desires: desired needs and felt needs, ambitions, needs which arise from competition and comparison with each other. Before all these, who can say which is too much?

When we spend less, when we keep only a little for ourselves, we become generous to others, especially to those in need. When we can learn to limit our own needs, be strict and stick to little, then we become generous. It is in this sense that we say: To be poor is to be generous; to lose life is to find it.

In our simplicity we become simple to ourselves and generous to others. The truth is that simplicity is a blessing and a value. But if our simplicity does not make us generous to others, then it is not a pleasant thing. Our simplicity makes sense only if we become generous and liberating for others.

Littleness and hiddenness can both lead to honesty and integrity. Honest persons are without fear or pressures from outside. They have no fear of losing anything and are extra joyful in gaining. When people are free from fear, selfishness, greed and ambition, they can be honest, authentic, genuine. They can be sincere and open. To be open means to put all cards on the table, with no cowardice, no hypocrisy, not showing more than what they really are. Only honest persons are genuine, authentic. They have nothing to hide, nothing to lose, no greed, no gains.

An honest person is an integral person. This is the secret behind the power of littleness and hiddenness. The most famous, most powerful person can attest to this. This is the power of powerlessness, and the greatness of littleness and hiddenness. This is also the main virtue of the Nazareth experience. This is a fundamental, a basic experience of the Nazareth spirituality: to live the gospel from day to day as it comes to us in simple, little, hidden ways. It is not pretending to be more than what we really are.

Silent but dynamic denouncement

Littleness and hiddenness are silent but dynamic. They are manifested in strong and powerful struggle to denounce social status and craving for honor, position and degrees. It is to live away from all securities, structures and status, privileges and power which institutions provide. It is to live the gospel without compromise, conditions and limits. It is to live the gospel before we preach or write about it. As Charles says: 'Cry out the gospel with your life.'

It is more than preaching the gospel in words. It is being the gospel, becoming the gospel. It means living the gospel in life before preaching it in the pulpit. It is giving birth and bringing the good news to maturity.

In our time, we often hear the slogan, 'If you want to live, display of power is the name of the game.' They bombard us with the thought that if we can have influence in the society, become famous and powerful, then we are living an ideal life. Unfortunately, this is not something that was invented in our age. It was practised even at the time of Jesus. But God, Jesus, Mary and Joseph, responding to the mystery of the incarnation, opted for the values of littleness and hiddenness.

SHARING AND CARING

In the experience and process of discovering and discerning the kingdom of God in the day-to-day life in Nazareth, sharing and caring is another important value.

Sharing is salvific

Sharing is a step towards attaining equality for all. The spirituality of sharing with someone who does not *have* consists in this: to the one who does not have I will give so that we can become equal even for just a moment. So instead of competing and being jealous, we will give and help each other.

Sharing leads to solidarity, feeling for the others, and compassion. Unfortunately, the English word 'compassion' does not convey the powerful meaning of its root. The Greek word for compassion (taken from the Latin words *com* and *pasio*) means to suffer together and to become a co-sufferer.

In Greek, it means that when we see the sufferings of somebody, something happens to us in our guts. Then we start to feel the pain of others within us.

Sharing is caring, understanding or carrying someone on our shoulders. Sharing is staying by and staying with someone. We are responsible for our brothers and sisters; we are accountable in carrying them up on our shoulder, in supporting them.

Sharing is generous availability. The best example of availability is shown in the parable of the Good Samaritan, his getting down from the donkey. We are all sitting on our donkey. We have so many donkeys in our life. We do not want to get down from them, like the priest and the Levite who passed by. But the Samaritan got down from his donkey, he stopped by. It means availability, accessibility and putting the wounded on our donkey and walking on.

Sharing is a sacrifice. Whoever becomes less, dies to self so that others can have life. It is accepting powerlessness and poverty in order to empower others and to raise up others, to lift up the lowly. So sharing is liberative for both: for the one who is doing the sharing and for the one for whom the sharing is being done. It is giving unconditionally, without limit.

Sharing is sacramental

The capacity to share and the spirituality of sharing is the effect and blessing of the incarnation and the resurrection. Why should we share? I feel that the more we believe in the incarnation and the resurrection, the more we will share their fruits and blessings.

By the incarnation, God shares his godliness, graciousness, godhood, and his fatherhood with us. We are privileged to become sons and daughters, children of God through Jesus. This is the blessing of the incarnation. Gustavo Gutierrez, father of liberation theology, uses a beautiful expression for this idea: filiation and fellowship. Once we accept the fatherhood of God and call him Father, Abba, we share in the fellowship of the brothers and sisters. Divine filiation and human fellowship are two related words. We should not dare call God Father if we can not call or accept each other as brothers and sisters. In this way, divine filiation becomes connected with human fellowship. What is hard to accept, of course, is that while being so related to each other, some of us can complacently live in abundance while many are deprived and divested of basic human needs. We have to do something about this if we truly believe in universal fellowship.

Divine filiation and human fellowship are really interconnected just as incarnation and resurrection are interconnected. The stronger we believe in the incarnation and the resurrection, the more we will experience filiation and fellowship, and the more we will share and care.

Mother Teresa of Calcutta says that the greatest evil in our time is indifference. Indifference exists when we dare call God our Father but we do not accept each other as brothers and sisters. The biggest sin against the incarnation and the resurrection is indifference: not sharing, not accepting human fellowship. It is a sin to say that we accept the grace of divine filiation but in reality reject and denounce the vocation of human fellowship.

Sharing is miraculous

Caring means trusting in God and others. It means letting go, giving up claims on others and putting our faith and trust in God and in his providence. It is putting ourself in the love and mercy of God, allowing ourself and others to grow. Sharing is bringing life to others and allowing others to enter into our life. Sharing means risking our inner self and our experience. It is bringing our life to others and theirs to ours.

Sharing is making miracles happen. Sharing is giving our loaves and fish so that the miracle of multiplication can happen. In a certain sense, the miracle of the multiplication of loaves and fish was not initiated by Jesus. Primarily, it was the work of the small boy who gave his loaves and fish. Secondly, it was not a miracle of providing fish and loaves in excess. Rather, it was a miracle of people-transformation and empowerment so that they could make miracles happen. We can work wonders and allow miracles to happen through sharing. So the agent of the miracle was the boy who shared his own self: his own bread and fish. The miracle was made possible by the others' desire to share in the life-giving act of this boy. In this way, we can say that sharing is miraculous.

Personal greed versus God's providence

Sharing and giving of ourselves to others is trusting in God's providence. But sharing is not always easy. Greed for personal possession and storing things for oneself creep in and become actually the biggest obstacles to sharing. Personal greed, therefore, is an insult against God's providence and a mistrust of God's love and care.

Paradoxically, in this period of capitalism and consumerism, there are more and more poor people. Even the richest persons feel so many kinds of poverty. Those spared material poverty undergo the painful poverty of not trusting in God's providence. It is not only material sharing that we lack. Even time, love, interest and concern for others are becoming less and less available. Persons are becoming more greedy, selfish, self-centred. They desire to possess and to have more than what they need, to show more of themselves than what they are. These people never have enough. They always want more. They have so much but they are always poor. They always have very little to share.

Today, people seem to want to be at the receiving and gaining end only. There is less and less giving and sharing. Those who only want to receive but do not want to give are like the Dead Sea. Nothing lives in the Dead Sea because, being the lowest part of the earth, it receives water but it does not give. Water stays and stagnates; it does not flow. There is no life; nothing lives there because it does not share life with others.

Mother Teresa of Calcutta says that it is only when you bridle your greed and limit your needs that you can become generous and start trusting in God's providence. Explaining her sisters' way of life, she says: 'We have limited our needs so that we can be generous. Whatever help comes in is for the people. We do not take commission for what we receive from others.' That is one form of greed in the church, we can say. When donations come, when funds come, we keep some percentage and the rest we give to the poor. To be generous is not to give only what is superfluous and what is in excess of what we need. To be generous is to sacrifice ourself for others.

Sharing is the locus of God's providence. If we share sincerely and generously, we put our own security in the hands of God. When we share we show that we believe that God will provide and care for us.

Recall that incident when Jesus was sitting at the temple treasury (Mk 12). We see so many people putting in so much out of their bounty. Then this old lady, who is not only a widow but a destitute, comes. In the text you will see Jesus talking about the teachers of the law and saying: these are the men who swallow the property of widows, while making a show of lengthy prayers (Mk 12:40). You will find Jesus condemning these religious leaders who devour and keep the widow's possessions.

What Jesus appreciates is not how much she gives. What is admirable is not what she adds to the temple treasury, but the fact that she did not keep anything for herself. She gave all she had, which is the essence of sharing. Sharing is not about how much we give but about how little we keep for ourselves because we trust in God's providence.

Sharing is celebrating the liturgy of life together. Whatever we share with others, we share with Jesus. 'Whatever you do to the least of my brothers and sisters, you do to me.'

WALKING AND WORKING TOGETHER

Walking and working together is being together. It implies standing and supporting each other in moments of difficulties and joys, in crises and crosses. It involves journeying together in the way of life, and moving on together. This pilgrimage presupposes standing by and with each other.

Life as pilgrimage

Walking together or journeying together is an important virtue of the Nazareth experience. The whole Bible, when studied from a certain perspective, can be called a journey. It is the story of God walking together with humans. There are crises, conflicts, ups and downs, growth, making and breaking of covenant. In the Old Testament we read of the journeys of Abraham, Jacob, Joseph, Moses, Aaron. In the New Testament, those of Jesus and Paul.

The letter to the Hebrews 11:14 says we are pilgrims on earth. This theme has been rediscovered and has been a favourite image since Vatican II. In fact one of the images used in the documents for describing the church is 'A Pilgrim Church'.

Similarly, the Holy Family, Mary, Joseph and Jesus, had a few journeys together. These were the pilgrimages of their life:

1. Some months after the annunciation, Mary went to the house of Zechariah and Elizabeth, in Ein Karem, the birthplace of John the Baptist, 3 km from Jerusalem (Lk 1).

2. A journey was caused by the census ordered by Caesar Augustus. Joseph and Mary journeyed from Nazareth to Bethlehem, a distance of about 160 km.

3. There was that long and painful journey from Bethlehem to Egypt to flee from Herod.

4. From Egypt to Nazareth. After the death of Herod the Holy Family were able to go back to Nazareth.

5. When Jesus was 12 years old. the journey from Nazareth to Jerusalem. There Jesus got lost in the crowd and was found in the temple. Nazareth is about 150 km from Jerusalem.

6. From Jerusalem to Nazareth. When Jesus was found, they went back to Nazareth.

Jesus and Mary had separate journeys as well. He went to Cana for the wedding and then to Capernaum. Then Mary, at one point, left her house and became a disciple of Jesus. She was journeying together with a few women. She was probably also there on Palm Sunday, in that short but royal journey. One important journey of Mary was the way

to Calvary. Finally, the resurrection and post-resurrection journeys
with the apostles.

Pilgrimage and faith formation

It would be interesting if we could walk together with Jesus, Mary
and Joseph on a particular pilgrimage and ask them: What was the
purpose of this journey? Where did they stop over? Who were the people who met them? What were the topics they talked about along the
way? Were they talking about their sorrows, joys, high and low
moments, bitter experiences, celebrations? What were they remember-
ing? In these dialogues with them on their journeys, our faith formation will happen (Lk 2:40, 52).

Making the pilgrimage was a yearly tradition observed by the Holy
Family. When Jesus was twelve, they began the journey with him but
came back without him. It was a very tragic experience. Mary and
Joseph were very disturbed because of that. It was not only their parenthood that was challenged, but their responsibility for the child that
God had given them to take care of. This child had really been giving
them trouble right from the very beginning! On the day he was born
many children were killed, and Mary had to flee. What a troublesome
child!

When he got lost, Mary and Joseph had to go back to Jerusalem.
They must have been accusing themselves of being careless in taking
care of the child. They presumed that he was with their relatives. But
he was not there. When they realised what had happened, they
retraced their steps and searched. They went back to where they lost
him. They looked for him among acquaintances and relatives, but they
failed.

In our lives, too, we can journey year after year without Christ, pre-
suming that he is with us. We, of course, know that it is dangerous to
assume such a thing. If at any point we realise that he is not with us, we
must turn back radically. This experience can be sad. It can be very
painful but it can also be very enriching and full of grace. If ever we
lose him, we must get back to the place and time when Jesus was still
with us, to that period before we lost him. Let us ask ourselves: When
was the last time that he was still with us?

'Why have you done this to us?' asked Mary and Joseph. They were
deeply worried. They were distressed looking for him. 'We are concerned about you; we are responsible for you; we are accountable for

you. Why have you done this to us?' And Jesus replied: 'Why were you looking for me?' Mary and Joseph did not understand his answer. We notice that whenever they come to the scene, they are presented as not understanding the whole situation. In many incidents, they just submit to the word and will of God. They don't understand. Not that their mental capacities are low and that they could not understand what was happening. Rather, they are presented to us as models of accepting God's word and will in faith. As it is written in verse 52: 'The mother stored it up in her heart.'

In this pilgrimage of life, Jesus, Mary and Joseph grew in faith. They grew in their response to the will of God and in understanding each other, each other's role, each other's mission, in supporting each other, standing by each other in crisis, full of concern. They learned more deeply the purpose and beauty of the incarnation.

An important point in belonging to a family, to a community, fraternity, or movement is the possibility of journeying together with others. In this joint journey, we grow and help others to grow as real persons as we feel the support, trust, care and concern for each other in joy.

Manual and menial work

Luke 2, verse 51 says: 'He went down with them and came to Nazareth and he lived under their authority.' Jesus went with Mary and Joseph and together they assumed their ordinary and simple life, their spirituality in practice and in action. He learned the social aspects of their faith, their life and their charism.

What work must Jesus, Mary and Joseph have engaged in at home, in the shop, outside, in the field? They were just doing routine, ordinary manual work. They were doing menial jobs, jobs that you would not like to do with your own hands, jobs that you referred to others if you had the money; that others would do for you – odd jobs, disliked jobs that represent low status and class. But in Nazareth, they did manual and menial work. The difference was that they did them extraordinarily well.

SOLIDARITY AND SUPPORT

Solidarity and support is the fourth and fundamental value of the Nazareth experience. In fact, it is a consequence of the preceding values and virtues. All of them are really interconnected and interrelated.

Levels of solidarity and support

Solidarity and support can be lived and shown on different levels:

– Presence.   Being physically there.
– Communication.   Being in love, in solidarity.
– Surrendering.   An experience of deep contact in giving
                         and receiving.
– Identification.   Becoming one. Identifying yourself with
                         compassion, feeling and taking the suf-
                         fering of the other as though it were
                         happening to you.

Solidarity and support is expressed when we love others as ourselves. The things we don't like to happen to us, we don't like to happen to others either. It is to feel responsible and accountable for others. To share one's shoulders with those who are suffering, in carrying crosses and bearing each other's burdens. To celebrate joys, hopes, courage and visions together.

Acceptance and correction

Mutual acceptance and fraternal correction is the concrete expression of deep solidarity and support. Love accepts people as they are, but when necessary it admonishes and corrects. Love implies creative and critical tolerance.

To explain this point further, let us go back to the loss of Jesus in the temple. According to the gospel of Luke, in front of many people and strangers, Jesus answered his mother back for the first time. These were the words he uttered, disowning and denying Joseph's father-hood: 'I must be doing my Father's business.' But if he were referring to Joseph as his father, then he should be doing this business in the car-penter's shop or in their house in Nazareth, not in the temple. Both father and mother must have been disturbed and troubled, and they must have corrected and admonished him. They must have put some norms and restrictions on Jesus: 'No, my son, it will not work like this.' Jewish families believe that sons must be bridled when they are young.

In these five to six days of the journey of about 150 km from Jerusalem to Nazareth, Joseph and Mary must have been discussing: 'We must be strict and correct him.' And it looks as though Jesus got the message and he understood. The text goes: 'And he came to Nazareth and lived under their authority in obedience to his parents.'

Fraternal admonition and correction is important and necessary, although it is not easy to do. But it is essential for us, being brothers and sisters to each other in a family or in a Christian community. Otherwise, the danger is that we may be doing things together without really becoming real sisters and brothers to each other. We may be praying together, working together, eating together, doing manual work, but without going deep in our relationships and in our commitments. There are many people who work together in factories, eat together in restaurants, but because they are not committed in relationship, they cannot have the courage to accept and correct each other.

In his gospel, Matthew says: 'If your brother does something wrong, go and talk to him alone, between you and himself. If he listens to you, you have won back your brother. If he doesn't listen, take one or two others along with you' (Mt 18:1-16).

Joy and peace

Working together, walking together, solidarity and support find their climax and are celebrated in joy and peace. When Mary made a pilgrimage to Elizabeth's house, there was joy in the courtyard not only among the people who were there, but also among those who were still unborn. John the Baptist was also dancing in his mother's womb. An extreme experience of joy makes anyone start to dance.

The gospel according to Luke stresses the theme of joy and happiness. Luke has ten different terms in Greek to express happiness and the grace of joy. For example, Lk 1:14 says: 'He will be your joy and light and many will rejoice.' To see the different levels of joy, read Luke chapters 1 and 2.

Joy is communitarian. We cannot be joyful alone. It is a communitarian and societal experience. It invites and unites. It announces the presence of Jesus, the Risen Lord in the community. This is the good news about life.

Holy Christians are happy Christians, whether they be priests, religious or lay persons. Disciples who are not joyful are far from Christ. If they are not joyful, they should reflect on their condition. It is impossible to be with Jesus and be gloomy. What good news can priests and ministers give if they themselves are not joyful? To be sad is anti-Jesus and it is anti-fraternity, anti-discipleship, anti-Christian.

There are two basic attitudes towards Christianity, discipleship and the priesthood. A group of people may look always at the crucified Christ at Calvary. They make themselves and others gloomy because Jesus is dead. They explain and preach to people that being a Christian is a big cross and it entails sufferings. A second group believes in the resurrection, in the living Christ. They are the more joyful group. For them it is a grace and a joy to be Christian disciples.

Prayer and worship

Prayer, praise and worship, according to Luke, are expressions of deep human joy. When we are joyful, we want to share the joy with Jesus and with God in prayer, in praise, in worship and in adoration. In Luke, every event is concluded by joy and praise.

The gospel of Luke, for example, begins and ends in Jerusalem, the Jewish universal centre of prayer and worship. The infancy narratives according to Luke, (ch 12) are filled with an atmosphere of praise and worship.

1. Zechariah offering incense and doing his priestly function in the temple (Lk 1:11-23).
2. Presentation of Jesus in the Temple (Lk 2:22-24).
3. The prophecies of Simeon (Lk 2:25-35) and of Anna (Lk 2:36-38).
4. Jesus lost in Jerusalem and found in the temple (Lk 2:41-50).

It is also very significant to note that the gospel according to Luke ends in Jerusalem with the atmosphere of prayer and worship and even of a solemn farewell blessing:

Then he took them out as far as the outskirts of Bethany, and lifting up his hands he blessed them. Now as he blessed them, he withdrew from them and was carried up in heaven. They worshiped him and they went back to Jerusalem full of joy; and they were continually in the temple praising God. Lk 24:50-53

Conclusion

We have discussed the virtues and values emerging from the Nazareth experience – littleness and hiddenness, sharing and caring, walking and working together in solidarity and support. To conclude this discussion I propose the following theological observations.

First of all, the most important and most difficult choice and decision that God had to make in the history of his Godhood was the incarnation, his littleness and hiddenness.

Abandoning his highness and coming to lowliness, the All-powerful became powerless. The All-holy and Most Sacred became human and secular. God chose and decided to be dethroned and be de-classed so that he could be with human beings. This is theologically and spiritually very important in understanding the incarnation and its implications for discipleship and for the Christian life as a whole. Unless I de-class and dethrone myself too, I cannot understand the incarnation.

God became simple, poor, ordinary and hidden in Jesus. He belittled himself at the crib of Bethlehem and at the cross of Calvary.

What a humiliation for God and what a grace for us!

Our second observation is this: God shared his whole self and incarnated himself totally and unconditionally, without limits. He became Emmanuel – God with us.

How do I feel about, and how much do I accept and practice, the grace of divine filiation and the vocation af human fellowship?

Finally, the authenticity of any communitarian living, family and friendly fellowship and fraternity can be measured only on the basis of how the values of sharing and caring are lived.

Walking and working together, living a life of solidarity and support are actually ways of contemplating the word and the will of God. It is contemplation in practice and a journey of life together which causes joy and peace in our life and in the society around us.

These virtues are part of the famous theme of Charles de Foucauld: *imitatio Christi*. Imitation of Christ consists in aspiring towards the likeness of Christ, to live in close intimacy with Jesus; being in love with him. It leads us to follow the Lover, to be like the Lover. It rests in being with the Lover and becoming like the Lover.

All these values and virtues are liberating. They liberate us from our harmful desires. Gandhi says: 'We are so enslaved by social pressures that half of our time, treasure and talents is wasted in showing off, and proving to others that we are big and great.' We keep worrying and doing what people tell us to do. We act according to the norms that people determine and lay down for us. If we can only liberate ourselves, we can be genuine, authentic and honest; and we can become our real selves.

Living out these evangelical values of Nazareth in our life involves us in a process of putting spirituality into practice within the context of our reality. It is making sociology our theology and giving this theological basis to our spirituality and to our Christian life. Spirituality made simple and close to people's experience brings out the social and spiritual implications of the incarnation.

o not understand the incarnation. Today, in our day-
ever we come across the mystery of the incarnation,
invitation to ponder and praise.

not understand the mystery of the incarnation fully,
nd praise. The shepherds did not understand what
ary did not understand; Joseph did not understand.
red, contemplated and praised before the mystery of
ke them, we cannot rationalise when we come face
stery. Questions and arguments make no sense. We
ntemplate and praise.

before the mystery of God's visitation. God inter-
God comes to us through places, events, human
sons. This is the mystery of God's visitation; and
ou can only ponder, contemplate and praise.

s when Mary came to her house. The shepherds
crib. God came to visit them. God became
ur sufferings, sharing our life, sharing our day-to-
ith us, dying a shameful death, but rising to ever-
. Looking at the cross, we cannot find sufficient
it happened. We cannot understand the scandal
nly ponder, contemplate and praise.

nplating and praising has another feature –
his is a beautiful theme in itself. So great is the
ting us that we can only be silent and still. We as
wly, so humble; and yet so great is the mystery.
oses is shown standing at the edge of the Red
aoh and his army are coming. Before him lies
an impending death in front, behind and on
od tells him: 'Be still.' That is the attitude we
mes to visit us. We ponder, contemplate, praise
. There are some other biblical references to
m 4:5; Isaiah 30:15.

ontemplate on the marvels and wonders of
ering that he exults us, the lowly. We shout in
nd in song. If we cannot be joyful, we cannot
cannot ponder and praise then we have not
tion and God's visitation yet.

PART VI

The Spirituality of Nazareth

Now when the angels had gone from them into heaven, the shepherds said to one another, 'Let us go to Bethlehem and see this
thing that has happened which the Lord has made known to us.' So
they hurried away and found Mary and Joseph, and the baby lying
in the manger. When they saw the child they repeated what they
had been told about him, and everyone who heard it was astonished at what the shepherds had to say. As for Mary, she treasured
all these things and pondered them in her heart. And the shepherds
went back glorifying and praising God for all they had heard and
seen; it was exactly as they had been told. Lk 2:15-20

Let us now look at other important dimensions of the spirituality of
Nazareth. We shall reflect on what Mary, Joseph and Jesus believed and
kept as their belief and spirituality. What made them believers and
what maintained them as believers? What inner power kept them
going, moving and journeying for thirty long years together? What was
their inner wealth and wellspring?

One of the famous books of Gustavo Gutierrez is entitled: *We
drink from our own well.* In his book, Gustavo is referring to the deep-
est spirituality and power within the person, in his society, culture and
faith. Gustavo declares that spirituality is always a power within. What
could be the inner wells and springs from which the Holy Family
drank?

The virtues and values we have mentioned have an underlying
spirituality. They emerge from a spirituality within the human person.
Without spirituality, these values will either be temporary and chang-
ing or they will dry up and die out. Every act that we do is founded on
spirituality and morality. In our every action, therefore, we must ask
ourselves: Why are we doing things this way? When we speak of spirituality in the period of Christian formation, when we analyse the spirit-

uality of discipleship, and that of commitment, we should not discuss behaviour. What people do should not be a primary concern. Rather we must look into the underlying spirituality, and ask: Why are we acting this way? It is only then that the real formation of the person and the transformation of society will take place. Then inculturation will take place too.

In the spirituality of Nazareth our aim is to be with Jesus, to grow in Jesus and become like Jesus, *imitatio Christi*. All these mean to act like Jesus, to think like Jesus, to decide and choose like Jesus, to get used to the way and practices of Jesus.

A SPIRITUALITY OF INCARNATION

From the spirituality of Nazareth emerges the spirituality of the incarnation. Incarnation involves listening to the word of God, self-surrender and submission to it, praising, pondering over it in silence, in stillness and in praise.

Listening to the word of God

The basic and important characteristic and charism of any servant of God, or any minister of the word of God, or any disciple of Christ, is being able to enter into dialogue, communication and conversation with God, with our own life. In this conversation and dialogue, the first act is that of *listening,* not speaking, not preaching. Preaching, teaching, propagating, are secondary acts.

This idea of listening to the word is symbolically expressed in the famous story of the Prophet Ezekiel, chapters 2 and 3, where he was asked to eat the scrolls. He was asked to swallow the scrolls and make them a part of his body and blood. That was a kind of incarnation, of the word becoming flesh.

Listening to the word of God is also obeying the word and the will of God. In obeying the word of God, the prophet must become word or the word must become an intrinsic part of the prophet's life. He must submit to the word before he could announce and preach it. This listening to and obeying the word of God is the measure of the authenticity of the prophetic call. It will gauge whether one is a true or a false prophet. The authenticity and the credentials of the true prophet lie in his/her capacity to listen to the word of God, to digest and be one with the word of God.

Asian mystics say that when the Lover and the Beloved become

---

one, it is like two differen
with water. Both lose the
third identity. They are b
not one is distinctly pre
risen to a new identity.

Mary, Joseph and Je
that of listening and ob
gospel in its genuine,
in them. They are pro

Surrender and sub

Mary, at the ann
word. Joseph did th
and not himself at
expressions of subr
places he emphasis
of Gethsemane, w
cross.

The idea of su
Jesus. It is very p
Jesus this psalm
Lord, I commer

Surrender a
God's projects,
ples. On the
surrender and
suspicions, h
with open ha
happen, 'You
prayer. Thi
Abandonm

Ponder

Luke u
ing over i
herds and
is that th
mystery
becomir
praise.

---

react otherwise,
to-day life, when
let us listen to the

Because we do
we must ponder
was happening; M
But they all ponde
the incarnation! L
to face with the my
can only ponder, co

The same is tru
venes in our life;
experiences and pe
before the mystery y

Elizabeth did th
did this before the
Emmanuel, sharing
day acts, and dying w
lasting and fullest lif
reason to explain why
of the cross. We can o

Silence and stillness

Pondering, conte
silence and stillness. T
mystery that is confron
human persons are so l

In Exodus 14:14, M
Sea. Behind him, Phar
the roaring sea. There i
both sides. And then,
must take when God co
– in silence and stillnes
this: Zechariah 2;13; Psal

As we ponder and
God, we rejoice in discov
joy and praise, in dance a
ponder and praise. If we
experienced God's incarn

Dance as an expression of joy does not consist only of body movement. It is a natural and spontaneous reaction and response to an experience of God's visitation and incarnation in our life. It is sharing with
others what is happening in our life, in joy and happiness. In Exodus
15, after the crossing of the Red Sea, Miriam, with all the women,
Moses and everybody, danced and sang their praise for the victory of
God. What God did for them mattered a lot for the people and they
sang about these with all their might.

And in the womb of Elizabeth, the tiny baby John, was already
jumping in joy. This is the consequence of God's visitation. We see
Mary singing the *Magnificat* too: 'My soul proclaims the greatness of
the Lord, and my spirit exults in God, my Saviour …' (Lk 1:46).

The first event that we experience in Nazareth is the incarnation.
We saw that its spirituality offers us different aspects and themes: listening to the word, surrendering and submitting to God's will and
word, pondering and praising and contemplating on the mystery,
experiencing God in silence and stillness, in praise, in wonder and in
joy.

These and similar features are present in Luke's infancy narratives,
especially in the three hymns: *Magnificat, Benedictus* and *Nunc
Dimmitis* (Lk 1-2). These hymns are explanations of the above-men-
tioned themes.

A SPIRITUALITY OF PILGRIMAGE

When they had done everything the law of the Lord required, they
went back to Galilee, to their town of Nazareth. Meanwhile the
child grew to maturity, and he was filled with wisdom; and God's
favour was with him. Lk 2:39-40.

Another dimension that we discover and experience in Nazareth is that
spirituality is a journey. It is a journey of life, a journey of faith. It is a
search, a perpetual quest for growth, for becoming ever new, for being
renewed and converted. Disciples are called to be lifelong travellers,
lifelong pilgrims. 'We are no abiding city' (Heb 13:14).

Experience of deeper intimacy
Pilgrimage does not necessarily mean making a long-distance journey to a sacred place or shrine. Pilgrimage is primarily knowing Jesus
through our daily experiences. But it surely involves a 'moving out' of
and a 'going towards' a new place. It is adapting some necessary shifts

in our outlook and values, even in lifestyle, in order to assume radical discipleship.

This was experienced by the shepherds when they were told that the Saviour was born in the city of Bethlehem. Leaving their flock they said: 'Let us go to Bethlehem and see the things that have happened which the Lord has made known to us.' They wanted to make a pilgrimage because of the message that the Lord gave them in his visitation.

The spirituality of pilgrimage is an experience of intimacy in knowing Jesus deeply. To be a pilgrim is to be with Jesus, to stay and to remain with him. John used the words: 'to abide, to dwell in him'. Brother Charles and many mystics will say: 'Stay with the Lover; talking is not necessary; just stay with him; journey with him, carry him, walk with him.' Recall the journey of the shepherds to Bethlehem or the journey of the disciples along the road to Emmaus.

When the first disciples left John the Baptist to follow Jesus, the first thing that Jesus said was: 'Come and see.' A little further on, after that experience, Philip then invites Nathaniel (Jn 1:46). Nathaniel says: 'Nothing good comes out of Nazareth', and Philip says: 'Come and see.' He does not reply to further questions. For the pilgrimage, no clarification is necessary; only an experience. 'Come-and see.'

We often use the expressions, 'Oh, we shall see,' or 'I'll see to that.' All languages have this expression. So, according to John, the word 'see" is not only an eye activity. It is an expression of the total person within; a deep experience of deep intimacy.

Emptiness and desert within

Pilgrimage is not tourism; it is not a picnic. It is a journey of life and of faith which is both personal and collective. Either we carry people with us, in us, or we do it with other people.

However, on the route to life and pilgrimage there are questions, doubts, suspicions. There are misunderstandings and uncertainties; there are ambiguities. There is an emptiness and a desert within that we experience. The feeling of being empty and in need of God's experience is almost a necessary part of an authentic pilgrimage. In fact, we cannot do any pilgrimage without these. But when we undertake this spirituality seriously and willingly, faith formation and spiritual growth take place.

On-going growth

Growth is essential to life. In fact, it is a condition and proof of living and being alive. Dead things don't move and don't grow. This is true for everything, for human life, for nature and for relationships. Persons, history, relationships either grow or die.

Kahlil Gibran, one of the prophetic writers in the Middle East says that love does not stay still. 'Love either increases or decreases.'

Likewise, our life graph never stays still on a linear scale. It does not go higher and higher, neither does it go lower and lower nor deeper and deeper. It always fluctuates. This is true whether in history, in a person's life or in spirituality. In the journey of life and in the spirituality of pilgrimage, on-going, continuous and daily growth and movement is fundamental.

Jesus himself grew in holiness, in wisdom and in age (Lk 2:52). Jesus is renewed everyday.

Growth is a societal phenomenon. It is possible only as a community act. Human growth is not an individual act. We grow together with and in relation to others. We grow only in society.

Human and spiritual growth is relational and mutual. We grow in the process when we help and facilitate others to grow. Growth is giving and receiving. It is sharing and caring. It takes place in family, community and in fraternities.

Hundreds of persons have shared, participated and enriched our life. From the hands of the midwife to the people who fed us for years, innumerable people have added and participated in our life growth. And because many have participated in our pilgrimage of life and contributed to what we are, somehow we are accountable to others for what we do with our life. In this way every life is a responsibility and an accountability. Hence, spirituality demands accountability towards family, fraternities, societies.

PASCHAL SPIRITUALITY

We saw how the spirituality of Nazareth and of the incarnation is a spirituality of pilgrimage. It is also a paschal spirituality. The paschal events include the passion, death and the resurrection of Jesus.

Paschal spirituality is basically an experience of dying and rising. In a simple and beautiful way, John explains, 'Unless a wheat falls to the ground and dies, it remains only a single grain; but if it dies, it gives a rich harvest' (Jn 12:24).

Paschal spirituality is lived through a life of surrender, submission and suffering, obeying God's will and fulfilling his plans. Paschal spirituality implies subjugation, abandonment and self-denial. It is an experience of emptying and going through the same experience that Jesus went through as described by St Paul: 'His state was divine, yet he did not cling to his equality with God, but emptied himself to assume the condition of a slave, and became as humans are; and being as all humans are, he was humbler yet, even to accepting death, death on a cross' (Phil 2:6-8).

Mary and Joseph lived this paschal spirituality. They taught and transmitted it to Jesus. It is clear that Jesus, in all the temptations, crises, and finally on the cross, surrendered his will to God, doing as his parents taught him.

Nazareth and Calvary

When we reflect on the perspectives of the Nazareth experience we see that Nazareth and the cross are interconnected. In the inscription INRI on the cross, it was not necessary to write the word Nazarene. 'Jesus, king of the Jews' would have been enough. But why was it used then? There is a contrast between the first two words: IN and RI. In writing both they wanted to express something: This fellow wants to declare himself to be the King of the Jews (RI). The cynical part they wanted to add was: But he is from Nazareth! Oh you, Nazarene, you would like to be king of the Jews! The cross is your throne! That is the basis for adding IN.

Though apparently cynical and satirical, the link between Nazareth and the cross is meaningful. There is really such a thing as the spirituality of the crib and the cross, of humiliation, subjugation, self-denial. In fact, no interpretation of Christ's life will make much sense without touching on these two experiences of Nazareth and Calvary, of the crib and the cross.

Fidelity to one is fidelity to the other. In other words, the experience and the way of Nazareth is the way of the cross. In this way the spirituality of Nazareth is a paschal spirituality.

Sacrifice of self as eucharist

To live a paschal spirituality is to follow the life of Nazareth and the way of the cross. He has said clearly, 'If anyone wants to be my disciple, let him carry his cross daily and follow me.' Those who follow Jesus are those who have received his invitation to imitate him in dying and rising.

It is interesting that John does not use the eucharistic formula during the Last Supper. The words, 'This is my Body, this is my Blood; take this cup, take this bread' are not found in his gospel. He replaces that formula with the washing of the feet and the command to love and to serve. For John, to serve and love others is to celebrate the eucharist. To die for others is eucharistic.

This is a very radical understanding of the social consequences of the eucharist. On this rests our contemporary belief that the eucharist is for human liberation.

Paschal spirituality offers us the Christian dynamic of dying and rising. It is the spirituality of self-giving. It is not limited only to a few pious acts and a few liturgies and devotional exercises. It is seen in the giving of self and atonement for others, in carrying the cross, dying, pouring out one's life and blood for others, redeeming and liberating others.

A PROPHETIC SPIRITUALITY

He came to Nazareth, where he had been brought up, and went into the synagogue on the sabbath days as he usually did. He stood up to read, and they handed him the scroll of the prophet Isaiah. Unrolling the scroll he found the place where it is written:
The spirit of the Lord has been given to me, for he has anointed me. He has sent me to bring the good news to the poor, to proclaim liberty to captives and to the blind new sight, to set the downtrodden free, to proclaim the Lords year of favour.
He then rolled the scroll, gave it back to the assistant and sat down. And all eyes in the synagogue were fixed on him. Then he began to speak to them. This text is being fulfilled today even as you listen'. And he won the approval of all, and they were astonished by the gracious words that came from his lips. Lk 4:16-21

Anointed and empowered

In this text we see Jesus preaching at the synagogue of Nazareth. He read a prophetic teaching in which justice and worship are linked and where the relationship of society and God is explained. It is a manifesto of Nazareth, the focal point of which is Luke 4:18.

Why was Jesus born? Why has he come? Why has he been sent? Why was he anointed? Why did the Holy Spirit set him apart? Why was he consecrated and ordained? The Hebrew word for consecration means to reserve a certain person or place for a certain purpose, to set apart, to be ordained. What is his mission?

His mission is to do God. To do what God would do. To do what God likes; what pleases God. Or to allow and invite God to act, to adapt the praxis and practice of God, God's way of doing things. It is not only to believe in the theology about God but also to practice the praxis of God.

To the minds which are so well-informed about the Medieval Ages and traditional spirituality, Lk 4:18 may sound too social and political. 'He sent me to bring good news to the poor; to proclaim liberty to the captives.' But this is what prophetic spirituality is all about and this is the manifesto of Nazareth. If we analyse the language of the text it does really have some political tones and nuances. These captives are the politically imprisoned and oppressed. This text uses political and not an ecclesial, churchy language.

This is supposed to be the spirituality of a Christian. Here we can discover the meaning and purpose of evangelisation: transmission of the good news and transformation of society.

Sent for justice and liberation

The spirituality of social justice and liberation does not consist only in doing social justice and practising liberation. Not in merely doing an extra exercise, or something beyond one's duty of being a believer and Christian. Rather it is a fundamental dimension of being a believer, of being a disciple and being a Christian, to live according to this spirituality. Believing and doing justice are not two different, separate realities. We cannot be at times believers and at other times agents of justice and liberation. Rather, it is in doing justice that we become believers.

Justice and liberation are integral to Jesus' prophetic spirituality. He denounced evil and announced the good news. He denounced sickness and brought healing. He denounced destitution and poverty and struggled to restore human dignity and rehabilitated people culturally and socially. Jesus showed us that to be a prophet means to denounce every form of evil, and to announce the good news in whatever way it comes. This is a spirituality that he requires from every believer.

Jesus opted for and decided to side with the poor and the powerless, with those who were despised and rejected, the voiceless and degraded, those at the periphery, the marginalised. Albert Nolan said in his book, *Jesus Before Christianity*, that the biggest difference between the spirituality of John the Baptist and Jesus is this: John the Baptist preached, cried out, lamented and invited the people to penance, repentance and baptism. Jesus took a different approach. He decided to be in solidarity with the poor and he went to live with them in order to liberate them socially, culturally and politically, preaching the good news to them.

In other words, he denounced death and announced life, the fullness of life. He denounced all that brings death, all that threatens and narrows down life. Denouncing all these, he also announced all that gives fullness and expands life.

The spirituality of Nazareth is based on solidarity with the downtrodden, with the lowly, the hungry, the homeless, the meek and those in prison. 'Whatever you do to the least, to the last, to the lost and the less of my brothers and sisters, you do to me.'

The love of God cannot exist where there is no justice. The love of God makes no sense if there is no justice. That means that the theology about God makes no sense if there is no practice of God. We cannot love God without doing justice.

The 'today' of God's redemption

While Jesus was in the synagogue, he read from the prophetic and messianic text from Isaiah 61. At the end of the reading Jesus said: 'Today this text is being fulfilled as you listen (Lk 4:21). What does this 'today' mean?

There are two words used to explain time in Greek: *chronos* and *kairos*. *Chronos* is the time which we read on our watches and on our calendars. We know it and we use it. It follows the routine of the lunar and solar systems. It is the time which we can programme and make an agenda with, which we can find in our diaries. We can plan and project *chronos*. That is why we speak of chronological time.

Kairos, unlike *chronos*, is an appointed hour, a definite and decisive moment. It is hidden from and unknown to us. It will definitely come but no one knows when. I can only wait and hope for it; I can only pray and prepare myself for its coming and happening. When it comes I must respond and accept it. God is the Master of the *kairos*. So I have to trust in God. It has not yet come but it will surely come. It is definite and decisive. It is now and at the same time not yet.

The gospel of John is divided into two main sections: the first twelve chapters and then chapters 13-21. In the first twelve chapters, Jesus often keeps saying 'My hour has not yet come.' But from chapter 13 he says: 'The hour has come.' This is the *kairos* of one's life: the fulfillment of a mission, the coming of God's person in our person.

This *kairos* is a decisive moment in history. It separates the past from the future. It is our *today*. Whatever has happened in the past has already happened. It is forever gone now. From today we start a new life. A definite change must be made. God is entering and coming to visit us in our history. When the time of God's visitation comes to us, a full and total response from us will make it *kairos*.

The *chronos* of our life can, of course, become the *kairos* of our life if we respond to God's invitation totally and incarnationally. Every day God comes to visit us. But if we don't give full and total response, it will not become *kairos*. It remains *chronos*, our normal history.

Kairos is a moment of grace within the *chronos* of our personal history. Today is the hour or the moment of salvation and the visitation of God in our life.

Luke likes the word and the experience of 'today':

– In 2:11, when Jesus was born, angels tell the shepherds: 'Do not be afraid, I bring you news of great joy; today in the town of David a Saviour was born.'

– In 4:21, 'this text has been fulfilled today as you listen.'

– In 5:26, 'we have seen strange things today.'

– In chapter 19: The visit to Zacchaeus, the word 'today' has been used twice. First, when Jesus was looking at Zacchaeus, telling him: 'Come down Zacchaeus, hurry up because I must be with you today.' Again, after the confession of Zacchaeus in verse 9, Jesus said: 'Today, salvation has come to this house.'

– And finally, the beautiful text on the cross in chapter 23:24. Jesus tells the good thief: 'Indeed, I promise you, today you will be with me in paradise.'

This time of God's visitation is a time of definite, decisive, radical conversion, change, renewal and transformation. The 'today' of salvation is very beautifully expressed by Paul in 2 Cor 6:2: 'Today is the favourable time. This is the time of salvation.]

Kairos is not the second coming of the Lord and should not be confused with it. It is rather the second incarnation, God's coming in our history and life. Accepting *kairos* is making our human history into salvation history. It is making sociology into theology. That means that our life becomes a domain of God. The human becomes divine and society becomes sacred and sacramental. Incarnation happens in our life. God's word takes flesh in us.

In this sense we hear Jesus saying that the kingdom of God is within us, present among us. We have to discern, recognise and accept our *kairos*. If we do so, it will cause radical change and revolutionary transformation in us, in our church and in our society.

The spirituality of *kairos* compels us to live the present. The *kairos* will come, it is coming everyday. But we have to prepare ourselves, trust in providence and have faith in Emmanuel. We must trust that God is the Master of our history and that he loves us and is with us and that he will make our life good news. *Kairos* will make our life joyful, meaningful and free from tension and boredom.

Today, however, trusting in the *kairos* is becoming difficult because of technology, science, watches and calendars around us. We want everything timetabled, programmed. In this age the spirituality of *kairos* may be misunderstood and taken as outdated and not a practicable phenomenon anymore. People tend to act mechanically like robots with remote control. Nothing is left in the hands of God, all is controlled by the hands of calendars and watches. We tend to become commodities of the market and not the masters of our own selves. Sometimes we allow ourselves to be used and exploited. But *kairos* happens when we follow the rhythm and calendar of God.

Jesus' words are actually challenging us today when he says: 'Can you or anyone make the hair grow?' Can your technology do it? Can your computers do it?

Let us not be attached to *chronos* but allow the *kairos* to happen. *Kairos* cannot be regulated. It is the plan and the agenda of God. It can make us experience insecurity and poverty of time, not being master of time. It results in a deep desire to be all for God. It makes us accept providence joyfully; it teaches us to wait, pray, obey and be ready to listen.

'Set your hearts on his kingdom first, and on his righteousness, and all these other things will be given you as well. So do not worry about tomorrow; tomorrow will take care of itself. Each day has enough trouble of its own' (Mt 6:33-34).

CHARACTERISTICS OF NAZARETH SPIRITUALITY

Then addressing the people and his disciples, Jesus said, 'The scribes and the Pharisees occupy the chair of Moses. You must therefore do what they tell you and listen to what they say; but do not be guided by what they do, since they do not practice what they preach. They tie up heavy burdens and lay them on men's shoulders, but will they lift a finger to move them? Not they! Everything they do is done to attract attention, like wearing broader phylacteries and longer tassels, like wanting to take the place of honour at banquets and the front seats in the synagogues, being greeted obsequiously in the market squares and having people call them Rabbi. You, however, must not allow yourselves to be called Rabbi, since you have only one Master, and you are all brothers. You must call no one on earth your father, since you have only one Father, and he is in heaven. Nor must you allow yourselves to be called teachers, for you have only one Teacher, the Christ. The greatest among you must be your servant. Anyone who exalts himself will be humbled, and anyone who humbles himself will be exalted. Mt 23:1-12

A poor people's spirituality

Nazareth spirituality is the poor people's spirituality. In the Hebrew language, they call the Nazarenes the people of the land, the people at the grassroots, in contrast to invaders from outside. These are simple people living far away from the centre of power. They are marginalised and voiceless. These are the poor peasants, workers, daily wage earners, of whom the parables of Jesus tell us.

The Jews of first-century Palestine were oppressed on all levels and from all sides. They were threatened by Jerusalem, the centre of the power structure, of the temple and the throne. They were oppressed by the Romans politically to pay taxes to feed the soldiers. The soldiers could get food from any of their houses any time when they travelled and patrolled the area to keep peace. The common Jews were also oppressed by higher class Jews belonging to the elite, the priests.

In contrast with Jerusalem spirituality, which is a priest's spirituality, the spirituality of Nazareth is a lay people's spirituality. It is the spirituality of the people at the grassroots level – the people of the land. It is a life-oriented spirituality, not a ritual spirituality.

The spirituality of Nazareth is life-oriented and, therefore, local, contextual, inculturated. It is a spirituality of the ordinary people. It is spontaneous, authentic, original, creative and cosmic. It is creative because it is not readymade and mechanical, not ritualistic, not bookish. Therefore, it is dynamic. But it is also relevant. It emerges from contextual realities and social experiences of life.

The spirituality of Nazareth is a liturgy of life. It is celebrated wherever life is. It is not bound to a fixed place nor a fixed time. The spirituality of Jerusalem is bound to a fixed time and a fixed place, fixed offerings, fixed dresses. Everything is appointed, determined.

The spirituality of Nazareth is celebrated in the fields, in the courtyard, in the lake, on the boat, on the textile shop, in the market place, in the synagogue, in the temple, at the wedding feast, at the funeral ... wherever life is found.

Nazareth spirituality is original, authentic and holistic. It celebrates with creation and the cosmos. It sings from the sound of the hammer of the carpenter. It is celebrated where bread is being prepared and bricks are being baked in the kiln, and where stones are being broken on the roadside. Where seeds are being sown and being harvested, where fishermen lower their nets, where parents prepare food for the family. This spirituality is celebrated in the struggles and suffering, in the burdens that poor people's bodies carry and bear, in the refugee camps and where communalism sows fear. This is what Jesus told the Samaritan woman when he met her by the well. God wants true worshippers who will worship the Father in spirit and in truth. Jesus was telling the woman that it does not make a difference whether we pray on this hill or on this mountain while the Jews pray in Jerusalem. God wants his true worshippers to worship the Father in spirit and in truth (Jn 4:23).

Liberative spirituality

Another very important characteristic of the spirituality of Nazareth and of Jesus is this: it is a liberative spirituality. Its primary concern is the human person and not the law. It teaches the values of love and justice, not the letter of the law, not norms and constitutions.

The spirituality of Nazareth supersedes laws and norms because the law does not respect the human person. It brings and causes death. It gives birth to sick societies. These laws prefer that society remains sick, so that the law can remain intact, safeguarded and respected. But the spirituality of Nazareth can dare break away from such laws which enslave, weaken, exploit and narrow down life. If life is at stake, and when human dignity is in danger, the spirituality of Nazareth, in order to safeguard life and out of respect for human dignity, will break the law.

The spirituality of Nazareth is liberating, not enslaving, opening the kingdom to people, not closing it on them. The appropriate readings for this are Matthew 23 and Luke 11.

Nazareth spirituality tells us that God abandons everything, even his own Godhood, for the salvation, redemption and liberation of human beings. God's action is seen in Exodus, when he listens to the groaning of the people in slavery, those who cry for help to him. He descends in the burning bush and tells Moses, 'I have seen the miserable state of my people in Egypt. I have heard their appeal to be free from their oppressors. Yes, I am well aware of their sufferings. I mean to deliver them out from the hands of the Egyptians,' and he said, 'I have come down for this purpose' (Ex 3:7-8). A similar theme is repeated with more emphasis in the synagogue at Nazareth during the first public preaching of Jesus.

God-centred

Every spirituality is supposed to be God-centered. The challenge of Nazareth, however, is this: which God is the focus and the centre of our spirituality? The God of the temple and the throne or the God of holiness and highness? The God of Exodus or the God of the incarnation? Is it a liberating God and the God of freedom and justice?

When we pray our intercessions, to which God do we pray? To the God of the temple and the throne; to the God of holiness and highness; to the God of the Exodus or of the incarnation?

Nazareth spirituality is not centered on the God of holiness and highness, but on the God of lowliness and of human persons. He is not a God who transcends history and who is above and beyond life, but a God who incarnates himself in history. He is a God who dwells and lives among his people, a God of compassion and of justice. Isaiah speaks to us eloquently of these qualities of God: compassion and justice.

Nazareth versus Jerusalem

In this section we shall not be talking of Nazareth and Jerusalem as two cities and towns of Palestine, but rather of two societies, two attitudes, two atmospheres and two spiritualities which these two places represent. They represent two trajectories in spirituality, both of which dogma of the incarnation that is important but the hearing and doing of incarnation in one's life and in the life of society. The biggest challenge to the church today is to be liberated from the preaching complex. Before preaching to others, she must listen to the word of God.

People today have no shortage of preachers. Communications media proliferate; satellite and cable networks link worlds which used to be apart. Neither do we lack listeners. People are ready to listen; there is a lot of people to preach to. There is no shortage of preachers and no shortage of listeners. But what people need today are genuine, authentic, prophetic preachers.

Incarnation is God visiting, entering and revealing himself in human society. But our world is too noisy and active, so that sometimes it is difficult to attain silence and stillness, and therefore impossible to hear God speaking. Because we do not hear, we are incapable of pondering and of praise. Yet, this is the only stance we can take if we wish to be able to respond to the incarnation.

In pilgrimage and paschal spirituality, we saw that we carry others along in the journey towards growth, and that the cross and Nazareth go hand in hand. Discovering one would mean embracing the other. If we want to discover Nazareth, the only way is through carrying the cross. Fidelity to one is fidelity to the other. Surrender, commending my whole life, whole self, giving myself for the liberation of others, this is paschal spirituality. This is also what the Prayer of Abandonment of Brother Charles is all about.

The spirituality of Nazareth is for the poor people. It is lay people-oriented. It has liberative perspective, aimed at the redemption of the oppressed, charismatic and not institutional.

It is also holistic. It includes faith, human life and society. It is creative, contextual, authentic, original, challenging and radical.

Today, it may appear that to be powerless is to be ineffective or it may mean to be uninfluential. But in its very littleness, Nazareth is great. In its very powerlessness it challenges the power based on structure. In its littleness it liberates people from oppression.

Nazareth may look frightening in being associated with the cross with death. But it finds its fulfillment in the resurrection; it is paschal. It promises life and life in abundance. To human knowledge, it looks foolish; to unbelievers, it may look like a scandal. But to those who believe, it is a sign of salvation (1 Cor 1:18-31).

Of course, Nazareth had its limitations. Humanly speaking, it did

can even co-exist within each one of us and in the community where we belong.

In the Old Testament there are also two ways of understanding the kingdom of God: one is represented by David and Jerusalem and the other one by Moses and Sinai. Those are also two trajectories in understanding the covenant. Likewise, Nazareth and Jerusalem represent two trajectories in spirituality. These two trajectories can also be applied in understanding the priesthood and discipleship: the Old Testament and the New Testament approaches. These two trajectories are very valuable in helping us evaluate the role of priesthood and of Christians in the church.

Nazareth can represent all who are at the periphery of any situation, whether of the state or of the church, and Jerusalem its centre. Nazareth is made up of ordinary, simple, poor people, labourers and farmers; while Jerusalem consists of the educated, qualified and trained. In Jerusalem there are institutes and buildings. At Nazareth, there is life, relationship and human persons. In Jerusalem, what is important is the law, the blessing and curse formulas.

If you do this, this will happen to you; if you don't do this, this punishment will happen to you. In Nazareth, the human person is the highest value.

In Nazareth, the basis of spirituality is solidarity; in Jerusalem the principle is alienation. In Jerusalem those who do the liturgy have a separate class – dresses are separate; things used for the liturgy must be separated. What is important are things, ratification, making things sacred. On the other hand, in Nazareth the people do the liturgy.

In Nazareth, spirituality covers the whole of life. In Jerusalem, the emphasis is on religiosity, performing devotional acts which are timetabled on certain days, at fixed hours. Once you have done it you are free of it. In Jerusalem one comes across 'religiosity' and at Nazareth one experiences spirituality.

In other words, Nazareth means charism and commitment; Jerusalem is duty and obligation. At Nazareth, we speak of lay people and liturgy of life, while in Jerusalem we meet priests and levites. In Nazareth there is a prophetic voice, while in Jerusalem there are liturgies, rituals and rubrics. At Nazareth the word of God is the power of the prophet. In Jerusalem, the structure and the law is the power of the priest or the king. In Nazareth God incarnates; in Jerusalem God is killed, murdered, crucified. In both cases those acts were understood as holy, sacred, in defence of dogmas and of God.

The concept of these two basic trajectories of spiritualities named after two towns may sound disturbing, discouraging and even frightening. But they are at the same time daring and radically jarring. They shake the roots of our theologies, ecclesiologies, liturgies They challenge our image of God, our understanding of the incarnation, our ecclesial structures and power symbols. They invite and challenge us to reshuffle our values and reorder our priorities. Jesus went through these difficult temptations.

Where did Jesus stand in relation to these two trajectories of spirituality? Where does our church stand? Where does our society stand? Finally and fundamentally, where do we stand as disciples, as believers, as Christians?

Holistic spirituality: The Our Father

Jesus often prayed spontaneously. The only prayer he taught the disciples, at their request, was the Our Father. The words of this prayer freely and spontaneously flowed from him.

Actually, it is not a prayer. It is an attitude. It is a spirituality of saying and doing prayer. It is not an act but an art of prayer. It tells us how to pray, not what to pray.

The disciples were asking Jesus to teach them how to pray. But Jesus gave them a lesson on spirituality more than on a liturgical or ritual prayer. What Jesus gave them was actually a programme of faith formation rather than a prayer formula.

Their request to be taught how to pray was not an arbitrary one for them. Rather, it emerged out of different reasons. Primarily, the disciples, being simple Jews, neither knew nor used any other prayers but the Jewish prayers. After staying some time with Jesus and learning his teachings and spirituality, they realised that their prayers were not meaningful. They were not relevant nor effective. So they asked Jesus: 'Teach us how to pray. How do you pray?'

Secondly, they saw how Jesus goes to pray without any book. He doesn't do the rituals: washing, purification rites, wearing special dress. During their prayers, the Jews had a special dress; they wore a small cap. They noticed that Jesus did not wear a cap, but he prayed. So they asked him, 'Teach us how to pray.'

Thirdly, they wanted to be good and faithful disciples. Any Rabbi and Guru would teach special prayers to his followers, to his disciples. Every saint has a particular prayer of his/her liking. Brother Charles de

Foucauld had his Prayer of Abandonment. This prayer summed up the spirituality, charism and commitment and key points of the vision and teachings of this person.

The spirituality of the Our Father is holistic. It contains the Nazareth experience in its fullness. The main themes contained in the Our Father are addressed to God, the person, the society:

1) The glory and holiness of God the Father
2) Daily human needs
3) Communitarian and social values.

God is invoked as the all-holy Father. His kingdom is desired, whi[ch] means readiness to do and obey his will. Then the person's daily nee[ds] are presented. This is the idea of the eucharist and of fighting for b[asic] human rights: sharing, equality, community and justice. At the en[d of] the Our Father the social needs are mentioned, as though it says [that] no person lives alone. No one can live in alienation. Every pers[on is] part of the society.

The Our Father also professes that spirituality is not a privat[e indi]vidual affair between us and our God. The person, being part [of soci]ety, needs freedom and forgiveness. We need to be involved in b[uilding] up God's family so that we can truly call God as our Father.

The Our Father begins with a proclamation of the glory a[nd holi]ness of God and ends with an invocation for freedom and j[ustice for] human persons. This is the same dynamic followed by the c[oming of] the kingdom. In this way alone can we experience God livi[ng in] us.

The Our Father tells us that God is holy. The society [is holy] but human evils make our society unholy. The day when t[here is] justice in the society, it will be holy and sacred.

The holiness of society depends upon the reign of ju[stice.] Leonardo Boff's book on the Our Father, with the perspe[ctive of liber]ation, is very important in this spirituality. St Irenaeus su[ms it up] so beautifully: The glory of God is the person fully alive.

Conclusion

We conclude this part by saying that the spiritual[ity of Nazareth] implies being with Jesus, growing in him, being like h[im. It has] different aspects: incarnation, pilgrimage, paschal and [missionary dimen]sions.

Incarnation is listening to and obeying the w[ill of God.]

not measure up to the mark of God. But still God chose it as the locus of his action. In the same manner, he anoints us, weak and limited creatures, to be prophets, to be his new Nazareth. The scandal of Nazareth in the face of human wisdom is the very power of God. What is foolishness by human standards is God's wisdom in Nazareth. Can anything good come out of Nazareth? Today we can still ask the same question about us: 'Can God work wonders in human humiliation and limitation?' To this question, God's on-going incarnation is the fitting answer.

PART VII

Nazareth re-lived

Bulls and goats' blood are useless for taking away sins, and this is what he said, on coming into the world:
You who wanted no sacrifice or oblation, prepared a body for me. You took no pleasure in holocaust or sacrifices for sin; then I said, just as I was commanded in the scroll of the book, 'God, here I am! I am coming to obey your will.'
Notice that he says first: You did not want what the Law lays down as the things to be offered, that is: the sacrifice, the oblations, the holocausts and the sacrifices for sin, and you took no pleasure in them; and then he says: Here I am! I am coming to obey your will. He is abolishing the first sort to replace it with the second. And this will was for us to be made holy by the offering of his body made once and for all by Jesus Christ. Heb 10:4-10

We have travelled a long way. We have journeyed together with Mary, Joseph and Jesus. We have visited Nazareth of first-century Palestine under the Roman empire. We began by seeing Galilee of the gentiles, the Nazareth of the New Testament. We saw events, persons, places. We witnessed together and experienced with Mary and Joseph the annunciation and with Jesus the denunciation. We also reflected on the values and virtues emerging out of Nazareth: littleness and hidden-ness, sharing and caring, walking and working together, solidarity and support. We reflected together on the spirituality of Nazareth from which others emerge: the spirituality of incarnation, of pilgrimage, prophetic and paschal spirituality. We also saw the characteristics of the spirituality of Nazareth. It is poor people oriented, liberative, God-centred, holistic.

In all of these we are actually undertaking a journey from information to formation and from formation to transformation. Information-formation-transformation, these are the three stages of our journey.

Finally, we can ask ourselves this question: What is the relationship between Nazareth and our lives? And we are ready to develop our final theme, "Nazareth re-lived'. In re-living Nazareth we shall discuss three points: Nazareth and Brother Charles, Nazareth and the diocesan priest, and finally, Nazareth and discipleship.

I LONG FOR NAZARETH

Brother Charles de Foucauld was born on the 15 September, 1858 and was martyred on 1 December, 1916. In the latter part of his life, he had a deep desire, a strong wish, an urgent urge to go and live in Nazareth. He felt an inner compulsion to discover the thirty years of the hidden life of Jesus. This he wanted to do by living and experiencing Nazareth. What was special in him was that his desire was not so much to live physically in Nazareth, but to let Nazareth live in him. He often used to say: 'I long for Nazareth!' He wanted to take and adapt Nazareth as a vocation, and to live it out. He was searching for a living experience. He wanted to take Nazareth as a charism, as a spirituality to be followed and a way of life to be lived.

Nazareth as vocation

Throughout this reflection we have been using Nazareth symbolically. Sometimes we refer to the geographical village in the province of Galilee. But mostly we use Nazareth in relation to the person of Jesus, as a gospel, an open gospel, as a value, as a charism, as a vocation, as a spirituality and way of life.

For Charles de Foucauld, Nazareth meant a charism and a vocation. He wanted to reflect more and more on how Jesus took the least and lowest place and how he lived in poverty. Here we are not talking about material poverty. The greatest poverty for God was that he became human, he de-classed himself. According to some exegetes, Jesus was not as poor as we have always thought him to be. He was rather a higher middle class person, not even lower middle class and definitely not the lowest class. If he was very poor, declassing himself would make no sense. Albert Nolan's *Jesus Before Christianity* is a useful book on this theme.

The biggest poverty we are talking about here was God becoming human, God de-classing himself. So he lived in obedience, in humility, in obscurity, hiddenness and littleness. As Charles would say: 'to pass unknown on earth like a traveller in the night.'

Charles likes to compare Jesus' life at Nazareth with that of the vocation of the suffering servant of Isaiah 52 and 53. This text speaks of silence, of stillness, of the servant moving onwards as a ransom, offering his body, his self.

What did Jesus do during those thirty years? What did that time mean for him? It meant openness to the will and word of God. It meant silence and recollection. It meant involvement with the neighbour. It meant obedience to the will and word of God. It meant penance, doing the routine and regular manual and menial work.

Brother Charles de Foucauld constantly sought to imitate Christ radically – inwardly and outwardly. He gave priority to manual work as Jesus, Mary and Joseph did at Nazareth. He attended to his guests out of love for Jesus. He used to say: 'If guests come, I will not only serve them, but I would like to grind, knead, bake the bread, and do everything for them because this is how Mary, Joseph and Jesus did for their guests.' He understood the Holy Family's attention to people in terms of deep, serious, active involvement with one's neighbour.

What is the basis of all this? How can such a level of imitation be possible? 'Love imitates and love obeys.' These are words that Charles often used. The greatest commandment in the Bible is to love. Imitation is its first fruit, the first effect of love. If you love someone, you will imitate him, you will obey. Your Beloved will be the only focus of your attention. He says: 'It's a kind of child-like love; a small child running, embracing mother again and again, jumping in her bosom.' He used to say: 'Looking at me, the people should wonder and ask: "If this man is so good, how good his religion must also be." And I will reply: "I wish you would know my Lord, my Beloved, my Master and how good he is."'

Brother Charles de Foucauld used to say that imitation in this way is possible if we read the gospel again and again. Read it often so that all the thoughts, all the acts, all the words of Jesus are always before and within you. You will then think like Jesus; you will act like Jesus; you will do what Jesus did; you will speak like Jesus.

Brother Charles de Foucauld often said that when you are in love with someone, you want to spend the maximum time possible with that person, in his fellowship, in his intimacy, just looking at him, talking with him, being with and thinking and trying to be like him. That is how he explains the value of adoration. And that is why he took

Nazareth and being in love with Jesus as charism, vocation, spirituality and way of life.

Cry out the gospel with your life

The gospel is very simple. However, exegesis, interpretation and homilies make it difficult and complicated. The gospel, well-read in a very personal way, needs no homily and exegesis afterwards.

'Cry out the gospel with your life' means to live the gospel as it is, in its simplicity, in its authenticity, in its originality and in its genuineness. For Brother Charles, Nazareth is an open gospel. It is very interesting to note that the gospel we believe in is about the years of Jesus' ministry only. And what about the oral gospel on the thirty years of Jesus in Nazareth? Where is this unwritten gospel? It is there in Nazareth. Nazareth is an open gospel.

Surprisingly, the gospel, although written thousands of years ago, is still alive. It is living not because it is written in the book, not because it is preached, but because it is transmitted and communicated by life to life. And it is being reproduced by, in, with the life of the followers of Jesus. This is quite an interesting mark of the churches in the third world, where many people are illiterate.

Preach the gospel with your life, 'Cry out the gospel with your life' was Brother Charles' spirited slogan. Such was the trademark too of the life of Mary and Joseph of Nazareth, who were silent and enclosed for thirty long years at Nazareth.

Prayer of Abandonment
Father,
I abandon myself into your hands.
Do with me, what you will.
Whatever you may do,
I thank you.
I am ready for all,
I accept all.

Let only your will be done,
in me,
and in all your creatures "
I wish no more than this, O Lord.

Into your hands I commend my soul;
I offer it to you,

with all the love of my heart,
for I love you Lord,
and so need to give myself,
to surrender myself
into your hands,
without reserve,
and with boundless confidence,
for you are my Father.

The Prayer of Abandonment composed by Brother Charles is a summary of Nazareth as vocation, charism and way of life. It is the summary of the Nazareth experience. It contains the ways of the spirituality of Nazareth, of the incarnation, of pilgrimage, which is prophetic and paschal.

The Prayer of Abandonment is full of gospel echoes, gospel voices. It offers great challenges. It unwinds generous openness to God, surrender and submission to him in prayer, eucharist, adoration, meditation and manual work. Let God do whatever, wherever, and whenever he wills in me. The prayer says to me, 'Come and see; come and follow him; come and imitate him.'

It is a prayer accepting providence. Abandonment and providence go together. It leads us to accept the *kairos* of salvation, the *kairos* of God, and to be open to it forever and for everything. It invites us to allow God to do whatever he wills, whenever he wills, wherever he wills in us. It embodies the meaning of listening to and obeying the word of God. It speaks of surrender and submission to God's will, of the paschal experience and of sharing the life of the Risen Lord.

CHARISM AND SPIRITUALITY

Then he said to his disciples, 'That is why I am telling you not to worry about your life and what you are to eat, nor about your body and how you are to clothe it. For life means more than food, and the body more than clothing. Think of the ravens. They do not sow nor reap; they have no storehouses and no barns; yet God feeds them. And how much more are you worth than the birds Can any of you, for all his worrying, add a single cubit to his span of life? If the smallest things, therefore, are outside your control, why worry about the rest? Think of the flowers; they never have to spin or weave; yet I assure you, not even Solomon in all his regalia was robed like one of these. Now if that is how God clothes the grass in the field which is there today and thrown into the furnace tomorrow, how much more will he look after you, you men of little faith! But you, you must not set your hearts on things to eat and things to drink; nor must you worry. It is the pagans of this world who set their hearts on all these things, your Father well knows you need them. No; set your hearts on his kingdom, and these other things will be given you as well.

There is no need to be afraid, little flock, for it has pleased your Father to give you the kingdom.

Sell your possessions and give alms. Get yourselves purses that do not wear out, treasure that will not fail you, in heaven where no thief can reach it and no moth destroy it. For where your treasure is, there will your heart be also.' Lk 12:22-34

Life in Nazareth is a spirituality that we can discover both in the family and in the society. It is a prophetic and dynamic spirituality. It is also contemplative, at the same time missionary and apostolic in zeal. These are the three main points which I see in the charism of the diocesan priest based on the spirituality of Nazareth: prophetic, contemplative, apostolic. Based on these reflections, I feel that the diocesan priests' spirituality fits very well with the Nazareth way of life.

Here is an ideal motto for the diocesan priests, a charter of their charism. It is in Nazareth that the vocation, charism and apostolate of the diocesan priest should be searched and understood. I think that the charism and vocation of diocesan priesthood was founded here. Diocesan priests must find their roots and basis here. Nazareth presents to the world a spirituality for diocesan priests: contemplation in action and vice versa, without being monastic.

He shall be called Nazarene

We read in Matthew 2:23 that Jesus came back from Egypt with his parents and that he lived at Nazareth. And Matthew says that this was to fulfill the prophecy that 'he shall be called a Nazarene'.

The title Nazarene was first applied to Jesus (Mt 26:69-71) during his passion narrative. It was later used to refer to his followers in Acts 25:5. Except for the apostles, all his followers were called Nazarene. In the Semitic world, which is more or less the Middle East now, the followers of Jesus were always called Nazarenes. It was only in the Greek and Roman world that they were called Christians. In Antioch, Paul calls the first disciples Christians (Acts 11:26). But in the Semitic world – Turkey, Syria, Jerusalem – they were called the Nazarenes.

The Hebrew word 'Nazarene' means one who comes from Nazareth. But there is another Hebrew word which is very close to it which is 'Nazarite'. In the Old Testament the word Nazarite refers to those who are dedicated, consecrated, set apart for God (Jg 13:5-7).

The Nazarite is miraculously conceived without human, biological efforts. The birth of a Nazarite is divinely announced, and so is his name, his mission and his life. In other words, the earthly parenthood is taken away and the divine parenthood is granted. The right of giving the name was normally the right of the father. But in the case of the Nazarite, his life, his name and mission all belonged to God. He is fully and totally of God, for God.

'You shall be called a Nazarene' also means being anointed by the Holy Spirit, possessed and empowered by the Holy Spirit. All the Nazarites work in the Holy Spirit. To be a Nazarite means also to be taken as the Lord's possession. If you are a Nazarite your life and your history is given fully to God. You do not belong anymore to your father and mother and relatives. Your choices, your decisions, your plans, will be directed by the wisdom of the Holy Spirit. It is not you anymore that lives but God lives in you. You will be directed by the wisdom of the Holy Spirit. The Spirit will be upon you and the Spirit will speak in you. To be a Nazarite means you are totally for God. Totally of God. Your main concern is to live God, to talk God, to do God.

This is a very important point for a diocesan priest's spirituality, for his charism and his being a prophet. It fits him well to be called a Nazarene: totally for God and for his people.

Nazareth and the New Testament Priesthood

Priesthood today is the most questioned, debated and disputed theme in theology and ecclesiology both in the First World and the Third World. But the discussions are from different perspectives and for different reasons and purposes. This is because contextual realities and cultural patterns are different.

Let me begin with a disturbing statement. Jesus was not a priest. He was a lay person. He was not a priest, whether in the Old Testament Jewish understanding, or in the Catholic understanding of our time.

He was not a priest from the Jewish point of view. His family was not a priestly family. He did not come from the tribe of priests. And we know that among the Jews, only those who came from family of priests could become a priest and nobody else. He was not attached to the temple as a priest. He never wore priestly garments. Priests were attached to the temple in Jerusalem for sacrifices. Jesus never conducted worship nor offered sacrifices and ritual in Jerusalem.

Neither was he a priest according to the present Catholic understanding. He was not pastorally responsible for a parish. He did not belong to any diocese or religious congregation. He did not baptise nor did he keep parish registers and files.

Nowhere in the gospel is he called a priest. He did not like this title for himself. His disciples or apostles never addressed him by this title. On the contrary, he was always in enmity with the priests. He had clashes, conflicts, crises, contradictions, arguments, disputes and debates with them. To say the least, it was finally the priests who caused his death. They crucified him.

With this background in mind, we really find it difficult to understand why the letter to the Hebrews calls him a priest. Not only a priest but a high priest! Why did he call a lay person a priest? In first-century Palestine, the letter to the Hebrews sounded controversial.

Reading the letter to the Hebrews today provokes in us some questions. What credentials, what qualifications did he see in Jesus, that he called him a high priest? What does the letter to the Hebrews contain that prove the priesthood of Jesus? The author gives some fascinating and interesting ideas and thoughts.

If we can understand the theme of the letter to the Hebrews it will help us to understand our priesthood as well, of which Jesus is the founder. It is also very important to understand it in the light of our theme which is the radicalism of Nazareth.

Hebrews 2:16-18 gives us the answer. 'For it was not the angels that he took to himself; he took to himself descent from Abraham. It was essential that he should in this way become completely like his brothers so that he could be a compassionate and trustworthy high priest of God's religion, able to atone for human sins. That is, because he has himself been through temptation he is able to help others who are tempted.'

There are two credentials, two qualification which make a person a priest of the New testament. These are being compassionate and trust-worthy. There are no other qualifications and credentials needed for the New Testament priesthood but that one be compassionate and trustworthy.

Hebrews 2:16 says that Jesus was human, not an angel. Being com-passionate and trustworthy, 'he is able to atone for human sins'. Compassion refers to his relation with human beings, his solidarity with them. Being compassionate and trustworthy mean that God as well as the people can trust him. He is true to himself, true to the peo-ple and true to God. Both humans and God can trust him in his responsibility and stewardship. He is a person for God and for the peo-ple.

What really makes a priest of the New Testament? It is not lineage, not the study of theology, not the eucharist, not the sacramental power, not administrative quality, not pastoral ability, not cassock nor parish. To become a priest of the New Testament, the only credential necessary is that the person be compassionate and trustworthy.

To be compassionate and trustworthy is to become *goel* for others. *Goel* is the Hebrew word for ransom and paying off the debts to liber-ate and redeem those in oppression and slavery. It is owning and taking away others' sufferings on your shoulder in order to liberate others. … 'Behold the Lamb of God who takes away the sins of the world.'

As the author of the letter to the Hebrews discusses the meaning of the priesthood of Jesus and proposes a spirituality for the New Testament priesthood, he seems to have an underlying intention of making a critique of the concept and practice of the Old Testament priesthood.

In the Old Testament, priesthood is based on the principle of alien-ation, being aloof from the people, staying at a distance, being set apart. Their lineage is different, their tribe is different; they wear dif-ferent kinds of clothes than the people; their time and place of worship is different. Everything in them is different from the people. Their the-ology and spirituality is based on the principle of alienation.

Why was their principle like that? For them God is a transcendent reality that human persons cannot contact. God is all holy. The sinner cannot see him. And no one can come close to God. Only a few special people are appointed and anointed to touch and see him. Up until before Vatican II our liturgies, rituals and the set up of churches, manifested the same principles too. The priests were away from the people, apart from the people.

In contrast, the New Testament priesthood is based on the principle of solidarity. Its spirituality is likewise the spirituality of solidarity, of incarnation, God on earth, God among people, God sharing his life among sinners.

> For it was not the angels that he took to himself; he took to himself descent from Abraham. It was essential that he should be in this way become completely like his brothers so that he could be a compassionate and trustworthy high priest of God's religion, able to atone for human sins. Heb 2:16-17

The Old Testament priesthood offered sacrifices of things and animals, while the New Testament priesthood offers sacrifice of self, persons, body. With this perspective we must re-read the text of Heb 10:8-10: 'the sacrifices, the oblation, the holocaust and sacrifices for sins, you took no pleasure in them; and then he says: "Here I am, I am coming to obey your will." He is abolishing the first sort to replace it with the second. And this was for us to be made holy by the offering of his body made once and for all by Jesus Christ.'

Jesus is priest because his way of Nazareth makes the New Testament priesthood. Jesus' way is surrendering, submitting, obeying the word and will of God, giving his total self, his poverty, his obedience, his celibacy, his body. So in the New Testament, what gives fulfillment to the priest? It is not the eucharist of bread and wine, rather it is the eucharist of life and of self.

This is what makes the New Testament priest: the life of Nazareth, the way of Nazareth, being compassionate and trustworthy, obedience to the will and word of God, submission to providence, being able to say: 'This is my body, this is my blood', 'this is my will, this is my choice.' Jesus must have said often 'this is my body, this is my blood' in Nazareth. Its culmination and climax was not in the bread and wine at the last Supper, but on the cross. When Jesus said: 'into your hands I commend my spirit', then the priesthood of Nazareth has come to be. This is also the New Testament priesthood. This should be the practice of priesthood of the diocesan priest too.

High spirituality and low spirituality

Based on these two principles of alienation and solidarity we are faced with two trajectories in spirituality also. One either belongs to the high or the low spirituality. The principle of alienation of the Old Testament priesthood gives rise to a high spirituality. It says that the people are simple and the priests are chosen, ordained, set apart. People are low, priests are high and must keep distance. Priests are no more lay persons. People are unholy, priests are told to go away from the lay lest they get contaminated by the sinful people of the world. People commit so many sins during the day; they are low, they are lay. They are therefore considered the least, the last.

But priests are up there; more experienced. They belong to the priestly class, the first among the many. This is high spirituality and it is based on the principle that God is transcendent, high, above, up there. Lay persons cannot know God. Only the priests are anointed and they will tell the people what God says. Priests proclaim that the people cannot see God; if they do they shall die.

In direct opposition to the above is low spirituality, which in turn is based on the principle of solidarity. Here we speak of a God who incarnated, who dwelt among us. We can know him; we can feel him; we can experience him. He became one of us. 'We have heard, we have seen with our own eyes, that which we have watched and touched with our own hands' (1 Jn 1:1).

The principle of solidarity is based on the theology and spirituality of *filiation* and *fellowship*. In the gospel according to Matthew we read about this filiation which is about God giving us the grace to become sons and daughters. Chapter 25 is about fellowship: that we among ourselves could become brothers and sisters. In chapter 5 God becomes our Father: he has graced us to become his children and heirs of the kingdom of heaven. In chapter 25 we receive the responsibility and accountability of being brothers and sisters to each other: I was thirsty … I was naked … hungry.

In the light of all these let us, therefore ask ourselves:

Is my priesthood that of the Old Testament, or of the New Testament? Is my priesthood that of Aaron or that of Jesus? Is it based on the principle and spirituality of alienation or of solidarity? Does my priesthood consist of offering of things or offering of myself; an offering of sacrifice which God does not want or of submission of total self?

Is my priesthood and discipleship that of Jerusalem or that of Nazareth? (Heb 10:4-10) Is my spirituality high or low?

Ladder climbing versus dancing circle

We have been talking about two trajectories of spirituality: one based on the principle of alienation and the other on solidarity. We have also linked alienation with the Old Testament idea of priesthood while solidarity is linked with the New Testament priesthood which is based on the incarnation.

To explain further these two trajectories of spirituality let us use two symbols: the dancing circle and ladder climbing. Ladder climbing fits those priests and religious who have a spiritual superiority complex. Looking down upon others, they are distanced, aloof. Seats and specific places are reserved for them. Only a few of them can sit in ladders of institutions and structures.

In the dancing circle all are welcome. Everybody has a part in it. We only have to widen the circle and everybody fits in. All are equally accepted, respected and are made to feel at home. *Agape* is celebrated as well as brotherhood, sisterhood, life-giving fellowship. One more additional member is a joy in the dancing circle. In the ladder climbing, nobody smiles because one more who comes is a threat. People are constantly looking upward for promotion or downward on others.

Incarnation means joining the dancing circle. This is the pastoral implication of the incarnation on our priesthood during the time of Jesus. The only problem of Jesus with the priests was that they followed a different trajectory. They lived a high spirituality – that of great privileges, lots of comfort and compromises. While low spirituality challenges us with values, high spirituality can offer us the throne and lots of promises. It is priestly, institutional. On the other hand, low spirituality is prophetic and paschal. Some persons in authority will prefer that we do not go into the dancing circle and into lay spirituality.

Nazareth is low spirituality; Jerusalem is high. In Jesus' time, the priests had their bungalows in Jerusalem and they had their estates in Galilee where they had their regular income and profits. The low spirituality can reckon the high; but the high can kill the low. It kills and threatens the other and considers this stance a sacred act.

In all this scenario of high and low spirituality, in the midst of the dancing circle or climbing ladder, where do I stand? Our stance will affect not only our spirituality but also our Christology and theology. What are my perspectives and themes for my preaching and sharing? What is my vocabulary when I address God? What attributes of God do I use? Do I believe in the God of the ladder climbing or the God of the dancing circle?

'Being' not 'doing'

In this age of competition, all is measured on the scale of success. Value is given to power and profit. Therefore, the main emphasis is on doing, on achievements, on quantity or quantitative gain. People ask how much you are and have. There is very little emphasis on being, on the quality of the person. But in history, radicalism happens deeply only when we do not measure how much people achieve. Fundamental radicalism happens only when we put emphasis not on doing but on being. We should remember people not by their achievements but by their being persons, their spirituality, charism, their praxis and the commitment they lived and died for.

We must remember that Jesus lived only a short active, public, pastoral, missionary life of three years. He was radical not by his doing but by his being. Such radicals have only very short lives to live. But they live forever because they believe that unless a grain of wheat dies it remains alone, but when it dies, it yields a great harvest (Jn 12:24).

The Nazareth experience is an experience of being rather than of doing. Doing is demonstrative. It is a temptation to do and to show. Sometimes, it is a power display. Doing is possessive; it aims to possess people, projects, power, privileges and profits. It gives birth to social evils like competition, jealousy, dishonesty, fraud, hypocrisy, and above all alienation. We can lose respect for life; we can kill a person for profit, gain and greed.

On the other hand, being means surrender, submission and openness to God. It is solidarity and intimacy and support to the others, especially to the weaker, for the sake of the human person. Finally, at this point, we can say that Jerusalem asked for signs and demonstrations of power while Nazareth did not give any sign; it became a sign. This generation asked for a sign, but no sign will be given to this generation (Lk 11:29-32;12:54-57). Nazareth itself is a sign. Galilee is a sign. If I want to discover, if I desire to discern the signs of the kingdom of God, then I can see these signs in the Nazareth around me.

THE RADICALISM OF NAZARETH

That is why I am telling you not to worry about your life and what you are to eat, nor about your body and how you are to clothe it. Surely life means more than food, and the body more than clothing! Look at the birds in the sky. They do not sow nor reap or gather into barns; yet your heavenly Father feeds them. Are you not worth much more than they are? Can any of you, for his worrying, add one single cubit to his span of life? And why worry about clothing? Think of the flowers growing in the fields; they never have to work or spin; yet I assure you that not even Solomon in all his regalia was robed like one of these. Now if that is how God clothes the grass in the field which is there today and thrown into the furnace tomorrow, will he not much more look after you, you men of little faith? So do not worry, do not say, 'What are we to eat? What are we to drink? How are we to be clothed?' It is the pagans who set their hearts on all these things. Your heavenly Father knows you need them all. Set your hearts on his kingdom first, and on his righteousness, and all these other things will be given you as well. So do not worry about tomorrow; tomorrow will take care of itself. Each day has enough trouble of its own. Mt 6:25-34

We have tried to reflect on the mystery, reality and experience of Nazareth. But what is important is not to know Nazareth but to re-live it. Together we tried to discover the possibility of re-living the radicalism of Nazareth and making it part of our formation. If it has happened somewhere in some hearts, then it is the work and grace of God. Then some moments of annunciation and incarnation have happened. Now we have to support each other, to take courage and to continue living out this radicalism of Nazareth.

'Following' not 'imitating'

When we speak of discovering the radicalism of Nazareth, or following the Nazareth experience, we must make a distinction between 'following' and 'imitating'. This distinction is from the last chapter of Jon Sobrino's book, *The Church of the Poor*, which is about religious life in the third world context, where he talks about contextualising charism .

Imitation means trying to do exactly, literally, physically the original happening. This is not possible in real life. Only film or drama can do this and only for a few hours. You know why? You cannot bring back the first century in the 20th century. You cannot bring back those Roman soldiers who were working around Nazareth. You cannot bring back their manner of dressing. You cannot find those neighbourhoods again. You cannot bring back the timetable of Jesus, Mary and Joseph. You cannot discover the shop of Nazareth, Joseph's hammer, the customers and the donkey. That Nazareth is not anymore available. In this way, historical imitation is not possible.

Interestingly, some religious communities tend to imitate their founders or foundresses until they meet some crisis. Instead of following the charism of their founder, they start imitating the founder. This is very dangerous. They start by eating the same food the founder ate, wearing the same dress which the founder wore and using the same furniture which he or she used. They become very fanatic, fundamentalist, narrow and conservative. The point is this: historically, geographically, humanly speaking, imitating is not possible. You cannot bring back history and geography.

On the other hand, following is possible and is necessary; even demanded. Radicalism lies in this – in following, not in imitating. Imitation is only fanaticism. Following means that you translocate the charism time-wise and space-wise. You translate the charism of the first century to the 20th century and the charism of Nazareth to one's own country.

So it is not a question of us living in Nazareth, but making the Nazareth experience happen again. Make Nazareth alive in us. Let us re-live Nazareth in us, wherever we are, in whatever we do.

While talking of re-living experiences we should avoid some extremes. The first temptation would be to romanticise Nazareth. This happens if for example we are living in the city and we get tired of it and we romanticise the village life. So we think that we must go often to the village, to a nice place .

That is not the way. We can go to the village but we also could be carrying our Jerusalem with us, and in us, in our being and behaving, in our thinking and acting, in our relationships with people. It is a way of life and not a geographical location.

Let me give you this other example which I read an one Indian newsletter. Some novices and seminarians were sent to an immersion programme in a poor village. They were told beautifully that immersion is a way of being one with the poor, of showing solidarity with the poor and meeting them. So they went one weekend for pastoral immersion.

While they were in the village, the people invited them for a break, to have some rest and food. So they went inside the house, but opened their bags, opened their coffee flask and hard boiled eggs which they brought along. And they started to speak in English among themselves.

How easily we carry our Jerusalem with us everywhere; and that is romanticising the misunderstanding about Nazareth. It will not be a Nazareth experience but a picnic or an outing. In fact, it is ridiculing the Nazareth of the poor people with our Jerusalem in our bag

The other extreme to be avoided is fear. Oftentimes we say: The Nazareth experience is impossible – I cannot do it. This is another extreme because it shows lack of faith in the incarnation and in providence. Remember that in Nazareth the rule is: no faith, no miracles. If I do not have faith, nothing will happen. But if I say Yes, even the impossible will take place.

The Nazareth experience is a way of life. It does not necessarily imply physically living in Nazareth. Rather, it is a spirituality to be maintained, a charism to be contextualised and a vocation to be lived. It implies tracing the way, the aspects, the dimensions of the spirituality of Nazareth. It is to discover our life at Nazareth or that our life of Nazareth could be lived and led everywhere.

We can live it in any place where it is most useful for our neighbour. It is a vocation and a charism to be like Jesus, to live like him in those thirty years of hidden life. His hidden life influenced Jesus' growth and contributed to his mission and ministry. And this spirituality of Nazareth made his life, death, his paschal mystery, possible.

Ab-normalities of God at Nazareth

Nazareth challenges us to live the gospel commitment as it is, without adulterating it; to live the gospel in its authentic, original and orthodox form. The gospel is attractive only when it is lived as it is; only then is it epidemic and contagious. We must carry it wherever we go and give it to others. We cannot but be contagious, evangelising, prophetic. Because of this, often it is dangerous.

Today, the biggest challenge to the church is to give Jesus to the world. Pope John Paul II, in 1991, addressed the priests in Brazil. He challenged and invited them to give Christ to the world: give God to us. Talk about God and do God and become like him.

But there are still deeper challenges on which I want us to focus our attention. This challenge is that we re-evaluate our theologies challenged by Nazareth. I would like to point out some abnormalities of the God of Nazareth. When I write abnormalities I like to separate *ab* and *normalities:* ab-normalities. These are ways of looking at God, not in the normal way we perceive and think about him.

These ab-normalities of God reveal the beauty of God – that he can act and do differently than we think and expect from him. He can be what is normal to us, but he can also take another step and be ab-normal. He goes beyond our human limits, hopes and expectations. He can be normal in the ab-normalities of human ways of thinking and doing.

At Nazareth, God is exceedingly ab-normal. He does not fit so easily in the holy dogmatic packages of the theology of that time. Neither can we limit him to our theological trends and prejudices today.

Let us present some of the ab-normalities of God which are in fact different aspects of the theology and spirituality of the incarnation:

God is ordinary and simple

He is extra-ordinarily ordinary. Ordinary in an extraordinary way. In Nazareth we see the human face of God. In Nazareth he de-throned and de-classed himself. He left his class and status and came down to the people. He risked so much that he was misunderstood and not accepted. He was despised, rejected and finally crucified. He was so simple and ordinary that we could easily miss him.

God is historical and contextual

The incarnated God is an inculturated God. This is a very important point for our theology, formation, spirituality and liturgy. He is not a foreigner or stranger to any culture or any context. He fits in very well. He loves and appreciates, admires, affirms, supports. He can be called upon and worshipped anywhere.

God is historical and contextual, he is not up in heaven, not hanging up in space. He is not sitting on a throne in heaven and watching carefully so that if we do anything wrong he will send some prophet as policeman to correct us. It means that he is concrete in time and in space, in history and geography. He is not an aloof and alienated God, not transcendent, a-historical or a God at a distance.

God in solidarity

The God of Nazareth is God in solidarity with people, especially those who are rejected, neglected, who are the last, the least and the lost, the oppressed and the destitute. He lives with and eats with them. He identifies himself with them. He is in the shanties, slums, among sinners, the unclean and unholy. The God of Nazareth is a God who allows himself to be dirty. He allows himself to be touched and he touched others. At Nazareth, a strange God indeed!

The Lay-li-ness of God

The God of Nazareth is a Lay-God. This was the basic clash, conflict, tension, and fundamental difference between the teachings of Jesus and the teachers and the priests of his time. Jesus proclaimed that God has a human face.

God is ordinary, simple, historical, inculturated and incarnated. He is in me and I am in him. But the teachers of the law, the priests, the temple-related and the temple-associated people said: this is a blasphemy. How can you talk like this against the all-transcendental God? It is an insult to the all-holy God. How dare you speak in this way about God? The teachers, the lawgivers, the preachers said: we hold on to our theologies which we have received from centuries-old teachings which are stored in thick books and our laws. Your way of thinking and talking about God is dangerous and threatening. This is a lay theology, a rough theology. Don't speak about God like that.

Jesus was saying that theology emerges from sociology, and that theology must influence sociology. In other words, if you want to speak about God, you must 'do' God, do the praxis of God in society, in human relations. The teachers and Rabbis in Jesus' time were saying: 'theology is theology. It is the domain of God. It is the holy domain and we are in charge and responsible for it. Don't touch theology. Limit yourself to sociology since it is the domain of society; it is profane. Leave the holy to us and live the profane. Keep the holy away from the profane.'

But what Jesus is saying is: 'Listen, don't call any person profane because persons are created in the image of God. Persons are holy; persons are sacraments; persons are theophany, the manifestations of God. By calling human beings profane we offend the sacredness and holiness of God. If you call a person profane then your holy God had become profane. In Nazareth he has become a human person.' The priests and

theologians must have silenced the man of Galilee by saying: 'Can anything good come out of Nazareth? Can anything good come out of the
layliness of God?'

We have to understand the incarnation well, and in this perspective. Our theology, which means our beliefs, our interpretation about
God, will influence our spiritualities, our priesthood, our missiology
and ecclesiology.

But we have to be ready to face contradictions. If we don't reject the
theology about God which we have learned from the Nazareth experience, that is, that God has become simple, ordinary, historical, contextual, in solidarity with the people, and that he has become lay, then
people will brand us as no longer believers. We will be considered as
idolatrous.

A proper understanding of the incarnation and of the Nazareth
experience will make our theologies contextual, real, meaningful,
effective, relevant and fruitful for the third world. The third world is
the Nazareth of today's capitalist society. And can anything good come
out of the third world? Can anything good come out of the poor, the
oppressed, the illiterate people of the third world?

Yes, they are the locus of the incarnation and of the good news.
They are the children of God. But they are so deformed faces of God
that nobody recognises them as children of God. They are the deformed
faces and deformed images of the incarnated God. 'Whatsoever you did
not do to the least of these, you did not do to me' (Mt 25).

They carry the gospel. They are the locus, the evangelisers and
agents of the good news. They cry out the gospel with their life. Yes,
the poor are the evangelisers. They will evangelise us.

They will tell us about God. They will tell us what is theology and
what is spirituality, and what is priesthood. That is why the poor are
the glory of God. We must, in our holy church, allow this abnormal
God, this lay God to be incarnated. Only these ab-normalities of God
will save us and liberate others.

The unaccepted and rejected God

What were the difficulties in understanding and accepting Jesus of
Galilee, Jesus of Nazareth? Why did the people not accept him? Why
did they say: 'Can anything good come out of Nazareth?' Why could
the people not accept the incarnation, the God of Nazareth, the God
in their midst? The God who is ordinary, so simple, so human? What

was the problem? It was not their fault. It was the fault of theology, of
spirituality, of liturgy, of the history that they inherited. They were
taught in such a way that they gave the people a different interpretation of God.

The first world and Vatican have difficulty in understanding and
appreciating the third world theologies, spiritualities and liturgies,
even ecclesiology and missiology which arise from a different interpretation of God. All depends upon what kind of interpretation of God
we have.

So these people in first-century Palestine had religious vices and
spiritual prejudices which they inherited, which were taught to them.
We must warn ourselves that religious vices and spiritual prejudices, no
matter how holy they may be or no matter how sacred they may
sound, are always very dangerous, even fatal. They are fatal for the simple reason that no one can challenge them. We cannot touch them,
otherwise we will be accused of being heretical, atheist, or even anti-
church. Besides, in the third world, if we say anything about religious
prejudices, instead of calling us anything else, they will call us commu-
nists or marxists.

The people during the time of Jesus of Nazareth also had their religious and personal prejudices and faith biases. They said that it was
only in Jerusalem that God could appear. God could not appear or talk
in Nazareth. Can any good come out of Nazareth? The holy places are
in Jerusalem, people should go there. Secondly, they could not believe
in any other God than a priest-God. They could never accept and
believe in a Lay God. They could only believe in a priest-God, one
who appears in a temple. God is present in the temple, not among the
lay people. Certainly, this is the explanation given to the lay people by
the priests and the power-based structures.

According to their explanation, God was so big, almighty, high
above and so much of a king, so powerful and transcendental. How
could they believe his incarnation in an ordinary, simple, humble,
powerless human way, the way of Nazareth? He was totally God
among the lay and himself lay! How could he be born in a lay house, in
a lay atmosphere and not in a priestly place? Every Jew would say: 'My
goodness, my heaven, what a blasphemy!' And the high priest when he
heard this, surely must have torn his clothes because his priesthood was
at stake. The chief priest was threatened and torn by a simple lay per-

son, by an insignificant and unimportant Nazarene. He must have
said: 'Oh no! this is difficult. How can a man of Galilee teach and tell
me what God is about?' So he must have torn his priestly garment
while declaring, 'He has uttered a blasphemy.'

The basic question is: Do I dare to accept the God of Nazareth?
God at Nazareth who is so ordinary, simple, so little and hidden and,
above all, lay? So profane, so social, so secular?

We can ask ourselves further:

How often have I torn my religious or priestly garb or vestments
when confronted by such a lay God?

What has been my response and reaction when faced with similar
challenges, with the ab-normalities of God?

These are, in fact, problems of discipleship. Do you remember the
teacher of the law, the Rabbi, the interpreter of the law who came to
Jesus and wanted to inherit eternal life? He wanted to make sure that
life was in his possession and that it would be everlasting. He asked all
sorts of conceptual, philosophical and theological questions. He was
theologising but not making theology into his spirituality. He was
believing in God but not allowing God of the liturgy, law and theology
to transform his spirituality and praxis. And you know what Jesus did?
He gave him no answer. He just told him the parable of the Good
Samaritan. Then he asked: Where do you stand? Go and become that
neighbour in the parable. Where do you stand? Do you act as the
priest, as the Levite or the Samaritan in the parable? Go and be neighbour.

There is a parallel story to this in Mk 10:17, where the rich, aristo-
cratic leader, an influential person, member of a leading family, came
running to Jesus. He knelt in front of him and asked what he should
do to inherit eternal life. He wanted to be sure; he wanted to know the
religiosity needed for the eternal life. 'Tell me what to do.' He wanted
to know some devotional exercises, some more pious actions, perhaps.
But Jesus told him to be simple and poor, to be generous and to believe
in the providence of God. Then he could follow the way of Jesus and
serve. On hearing this, he was filled with sadness and went away.

After he went away, Jesus continued to speak: Don't be so foolish as
to push the camel into the needle's eye. One can try and it is possible
that one day one might succeed. What Jesus is saying here is that a rich
man entering his kingdom remains an impossibility. It will, by itself,

be a miracle for a rich man to be converted and to enter God's kingdom.

Still another example of conflict and crisis which people face in discipleship is the story of Nicodemus (Jn 3). Nicodemus, leader and teacher of the people of Israel, comes to Jesus secretly at night to have a little sharing. He comes for reflection, and to make a retreat, a u-turn. In the gospel according to John, night and darkness have special meaning and theological significance. Nicodemus had a strong urge to know, to share, to do things better. And we know how the rest of the story goes.

'What shall I do to inherit eternal life?' asked Nicodemus. Jesus told him: 'Unless a man is born again, he cannot enter the kingdom of God.'

Go back to Galilee

After the resurrection, in his first appearance in the garden, Jesus told Magdalene to 'Go back to Galilee; there I shall see them, meet them. Get back to Galilee.' This was the message on the morning of the resurrection to the Galilee of the gentiles.

And there, coming to meet them, was Jesus. 'Greetings' he said. And the women came up to him and, falling down before him, clasped his feet. Then Jesus said to them, 'Do not be afraid; go and tell my brothers that they must leave for Galilee; they will see me there'. Mt 28:9-10

What does this 'going back to Galilee' mean? It is a complete turning back, a conversion, a renewed understanding of the person and mission of Jesus of Nazareth. It is important to go back where we began. It is necessary to go back to Galilee and re-evaluate our theology, our christology, our spirituality, our liturgy. We need to get a new understanding of Jesus.

Today, traditional theology is of no use to the third world. It is not relevant nor effective. Only when theology becomes spirituality, will our faith in God and our talk about God become our praxis of God. If we follow Jesus, then we can truly understand his reality.

So the invitation of the Risen Lord to Mary of Magdala was to go back to Galilee. There, they shall see him; there they will experience him. The people ridiculed Nazareth. Jerusalem ridiculed, insulted and even killed Jesus of Nazareth. But in doing so, they accepted and confessed the radicalism of Nazareth. So in their acceptance and rejection, they were radicalising the experience and practice of Nazareth more and more. Nazareth life and experience is radically challenging.

What is my response to it? It is difficult; but it is not impossible. Jesus is the Master of the Impossible. Personally, I realise that so many of the conflicts and crisis in my priesthood, and the impossibilities which I faced in my theological and priestly life, are not new. The people at Nazareth, the people at Jerusalem, the people in the time of Jesus also faced those problems. Mary, Joseph, Jesus also went through this process.

There are so many models of radical disciples, who faced crisis and conflicts in following Christ. There is a constant invitation to 'go back to Galilee'. There, one will experience what Nazareth meant for Jesus, Mary and Joseph; what Nazareth meant for the Little Brothers, for Brother Charles, for the religious and priestly life and for the disciples of Jesus.

Conclusion

Nazareth is an invitation, a demand, a model for diocesan priesthood and for all Christians. The Nazareth experience, spirituality and way of life are significant for the third world perspective in its solidarity with the poor.

The oppressed people are praying and crying for the God of the Exodus and the God of the incarnation. The poor are crying out so that the God of the Exodus may descend again and that some bush may burn again. They are crying out for the God of Nazareth, for the God who incarnated in Nazareth to be incarnated again in the third world.

The oppressed people of the third world are waiting, hoping, for their *kairos* of liberation, *kairos* of redemption. They have waited enough. They are in urgent and real need of a prophetic practice and spirituality like that of Nazareth, like that of Jesus. Such spirituality needs to be inculturated. It must be local, with and for the people. It will be prophetic, paschal, liberative.

We need such *kairos*. We should pray that such Nazareth may happen in our priesthood, in our religious life, in our spirituality and in our discipleship. We need Nazareth in our church, in our societies, in our world.